With Best Wishes

March 18 2015

Walter & Richard.

Thanks for all your help!

THE QUEEN AND THE U.S.A.

July 1976, Philadelphia, USA, Her Majesty Queen Elizabeth II with His Royal Highness The Prince Phillip, Duke of Edinburgh inspect the Liberty Bell, a symbol of American Independence. Photo by Rolls Press/Popperfoto/Getty Images

This scene is one that neither the Founding Fathers, nor King George III, could have ever imagined, but it happened. Why? Because a hereditary monarchy has come to symbolize liberty and the Great Republic has been its main defender. It is a magical symmetry, an unpredictable synthesis, and continues to shape the future.

The Queen's Diamond Jubilee represents not just 60 years of a special relationship, but 400.

First Printing
Copyright © 2012

Co-Authors
The Lord Watson of Richmond, CBE and H. Edward Mann

Publisher
Wayne Dementi
Dementi Milestone Publishing, Inc.
Manakin-Sabot, VA 23103
www.dementimilestonepublishing.com

Cataloging-in-publication data for this book is available from
The Library of Congress.
ISBN: 978-0-9838348-9-2

Graphic design by:
Jayne E. Hushen
Dementi Milestone Publishing, Inc.

Proofreading and Administration by:
Ellen LeCompte
Richmond, Virginia

Research and editorial support by:
Will Mann
Aynsley Fisher

Printed in the USA

Attempts have been made to identify the owners of all copyrighted materials appearing in this book. The book team extends their apology for any errors or omissions and encourage copyright owners inadvertently missed to contact them.

DEDICATION

*To all peoples of Great Britain and the United States of America
who believe in, and treasure, the democratic values that define
the special relationship between*

"THE QUEEN AND
Celebrating the Democratic Legacies th

PROLOGUE

This volume contains a series of essays on the common values that underlie the political institutions of Great Britain and the United States. These writings are designed as brief stand-alone commentaries to review common connections and motivate the reader to review individual topics. Also, when taken as a whole, they provide a glimpse into the unique reliance American political institutions owe to English ideas and frameworks.

In addition to these essays, there is some reflection - as well as a series of photo essays - on the visits to Virginia by Her Majesty Queen Elizabeth II to celebrate those shared democratic values, as well as photos of two groups of Virginians going to England to further commemorate these ties. They show in a graphic and colorful manner that, with more than 50 years of visits and events, the Queen has enhanced and reconfirmed these underlying democratic values.

It is ironic that when reviewing photos from the various visits of the Queen, one sees Americans taking pains to best present their own values. Similar to a child's reaction while performing at a piano recital - "Yes, Mom – you see, I have been paying attention during all those lessons" there is almost an overt pride when displaying what has been grasped and later applied.

Democracy is not a final product - it is a process. Democracy can never be perfected, due in part to the flaws in human nature, as well as the never-ending array of unique circumstances that confront the body politic. However, there are timeless components of liberty and freedom that need inclusion in any political framework that claims to be democratic. These components include: 1) the rule of law, 2) representative government, 3) free markets, and 4) respect for diversity.

The study of the evolution of British structures in America, which began in Virginia over 400 years ago, provides a look into the very nature of democracy. As a proud Virginian, I am humbled to say that the Commonwealth of Virginia has held an important role in building the special relationship. Her Majesty's three visits to Virginia over that the past 55 years and her support of America over the past 60 years add continuity and context to the durability of these values.

Lord Watson and I are extremely grateful to the following authors who have graciously contributed their expertise and insights for this book:

• We are honored to have a Forward by Justice Sandra Day O'Connor, Retired Associate Justice of the United States Supreme Court. Her lifetime of service to her country continues with various and numerous efforts, whether she is serving as Chancellor to the College of William and Mary, her incredible involvement in 2007 as Honorary Chair of the 400th Anniversary of Jamestown, or her continuing efforts to push for more productive civics education in the US.

• Although born into the British Royal family, Her Majesty Queen Elizabeth II was not in direct line to ascend to the throne. In other words, during her early life, it was not assumed she would be Queen. Additionally, her childhood played out when bombs dropped on London in World War II, with neither the East End of London nor Buckingham Palace being immune. It is therefore useful to reflect on her formative years and an essay by Dr. James Kelly, former Director of Museums of the Virginia Historical Society, raises some interesting points re: her upbringing and her childhood.

• My essay focuses on how early settlers, and later colonists, wrestled with the circumstances of structuring Virginia political intuitions using British templates. I also comment on how, during the 174 years from settlement in Jamestown to the Revolution's end at Yorktown, the American continent became a breeding ground for

ment in Jamestown to the Revolution's end at Yorktown, the American continent became a breeding ground for new permutations on old political themes.

• My co-author, Lord Watson of Richmond, CBE, a member of the British House of Lords, advisor to European business leaders and well-known commentator on the world situation, has written an expansive and fascinating essay on how the global spread of democracy is directly connected to the spread of the use of the English language across the world.

• The highly respected historian of the Virginia colonial period Dr. Warren M. Billings, Chairman Emeritus of the Department of History at the University of New Orleans, provides his expertise to explain how and why the General Assembly of Virginia, created in 1619, evolved into a body both recognizable for it parliamentary roots, yet different from its British predecessor.

• The Rt. Hon. Lord Howell of Guildford, currently Minister of State for the British Foreign and Commonwealth Office, talks about the importance of the British Commonwealth and how it is an institution that shares British and American democratic values. He also reminds us that it could be utilized as a vehicle for strengthening and expanding freedom around the world.

• In a short yet powerful essay, author, legal scholar and federal Judge J. Harvie Wilkinson examines the concept of the rule of law, pointing that it - rather than individuals or the accumulation of power - is the cornerstone of liberty for citizens in both the US and UK.

• Respected business leader Richard Olver, currently Chairman of BAE Systems, addresses the topical subject of market structures and business concepts shared by the UK and US. He briefly highlights the common threads of entrepreneurialism, free markets, and global trade and then draws attention to the dynamics of governmental intervention in current economic systems.

• While respecting and complimenting British and American political ideals, well known Native American historian and commentator Karenne Wood writes on the lack of respect for diversity that occurred in the commemorations prior to 2007. In that vein, she asks questions about whether the events of the past 400 years were inevitable and/or just.

• In the final essay, I write about the future of the 'special relationship'. Included in this is a call to focus effective civic education to students of all ages across the globe. As an advisor to Prof. Larry Sabato at the University of Virginia Center for Politics, I have had the chance to review recent developments re: the growth of democracy in a complicated world. Only vigorous domestic and international efforts will assure that freedoms won with the blood and efforts of the special relationship do not slip away.

Although these essays are of different styles, lengths and focus, they provide an accessible perspective on the important foundations of Anglo American political thought. This book has been published to commemorate The Queen's Diamond Jubilee and use the associated events as a touchstone reminding citizens around the world of The Queen's efforts to highlight and facilitate democracy around the world.

Horace Edward Mann
Richmond Virginia (USA)
January 2012

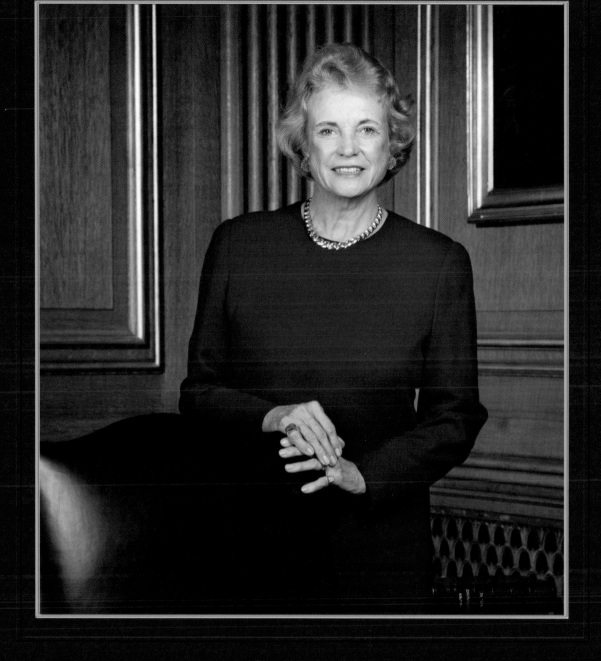

SANDRA DAY O'CONNOR

Associate Justice of the United States Supreme Court (retired), was born in El Paso, Texas, March 26, 1930. She married John Jay O'Connor III in 1952 and has three sons - Scott, Brian, and Jay. She received her B.A. and LL.B. from Stanford University. She served as Deputy County Attorney of San Mateo County, California from 1952–1953 and as a civilian attorney for Quartermaster Market Center, Frankfurt, Germany from 1954–1957. From 1958–1960, she practiced law in Maryvale, Arizona, and served as Assistant Attorney General of Arizona from 1965–1969. She was appointed to the Arizona State Senate in1969 and was subsequently reelected to two two-year terms. In 1975 she was elected Judge of the Maricopa County Superior Court and served until 1979, when she was appointed to the Arizona Court of Appeals. President Reagan nominated her as an Associate Justice of the Supreme Court, and she took her seat September 25, 1981. Justice O'Connor retired from the Supreme Court on January 31, 2006.

FOREWORD

by

Sandra Day O'Connor

The first permanent English Settlement in North America, established in May 1607 on the banks of the James River, was an event that changed the world. The settlers planted in the rich Virginia soil the English language, law and culture along with their crops, and from this brave settlement the United States of America was born. Many of our country's institutions, and those of other mature and emerging democracies around the world, trace their roots to this seminal event when the Old and New Worlds came together.

The settlers who cultivated the successful colony at Jamestown brought with them, by charter, the rights of Englishmen and a heritage of liberty and of the rule of law as grounded in the Magna Carta. A dozen years after the settlers' first arrival on Jamestown's shore – and before the arrival of Pilgrims at Plymouth – the Virginians convened the first elected assembly in America, an exercise of representative democracy that has continued, uninterrupted, to the present day. Thus the democracies movement that is sweeping the globe in our time traces its origin to some English antecedents of freedom and democratic practices tested and modified in America. The Virginia colony was the incubator for the ideas and the statesmen who forged many democratic institutions that are in use round the world today. That experiment in democracy continues to define the character of our two nations and is bringing self-determination to peoples around the world.

The commemorations of Jamestown continued a tradition of great American and British celebrations to mark special moments in our shared history. In 1907, President Theodore Roosevelt led an international exposition to Jamestown and declared that the "founding of Jamestown marks the beginning of the history of the United States of America."

Visiting the United States eight times during her sixty year reign, Her Majesty Queen Elizabeth II has made three visits to Virginia to observe and to commemorate our strong mutual interests and our shared beliefs – one in 1957, one in 1976, and one in 2007. On each occasion, many Americans were privileged to see Queen Elizabeth II and the Duke of Edinburgh and to observe their dignity, gracious demeanor and their response to American friends. Their visits have promoted the study and appreciation of our long term connections, our shared history, and our common values.

This remarkable book reminds all of us of these events and of our continued close connections spanning several centuries and manifested in so many ways still today.

Sandra Day O'Connor

GERALD R. FORD, 1976

Gerald Ford (1913-2006) 38th President of the United States 1974-1977, dancing with Queen Elizabeth II at the ball at the White House, Washington, during the 1976 Bicentennial Celebrations of the Declaration of Independence. Photo by Universal History Archive/Getty Images

Queen Elizabeth has met personally with twelve U.S. Presidents. During the 1950s, she was photographed with President Truman (while still a princess,) future President Nixon, former President Hoover and President Eisenhower. In 1961, she hosted President and Jacqueline Kennedy at Buckingham Palace. In 1976, she visited with President Ford during the Bicentennial Celebrations of the Declaration of Independence and later with President Carter at Buckingham Palace. In 1982, she hosted President Reagan at Windsor Castle where they were photographed riding together. In 1991, she visited with President George H.W. Bush at the White House. In 2000, she hosted President Clinton and his family for a visit to Buckingham Palace, and in 2007, she was photographed with President George W. Bush in Washington, D.C. In 2011, President Obama visited with her at Buckingham Palace.

It is fair to say this is indeed a remarkable accomplishment, and with the exception of President Lyndon B. Johnson, she has met with every President of the United States since 1951.

HERBERT H. HOOVER
WALDORF ASTORIA, NEW YORK
OCTOBER 21, 1957

Queen Elizabeth II addresses more than 2,000 persons at an official city luncheon at the hotel Waldorf-Astoria, New York on Oct. 21, 1957. Flanking her are former President Herbert Hoover, left, and New York City's Mayor Robert Wagner. Seated behind her are, from left: Sen. Jacob Javits (R-NY), Mrs. Franklin D. Roosevelt, Sen. Irving Ives (R-NY) and Maj. S.K. Anthony of Ghana. AP Photo

HARRY S. TRUMAN
NOVEMBER 1, 1951

Princess Elizabeth and President Harry Truman sit for this picture in the Canadian Embassy in Washington, on Nov. 1, 1951 during formal dinner for the Trumans. The Princess and her husband, the Duke of Edinburgh, played host to the Trumans. This was one of the high spots of the royal couple's Washington visit which followed their Canadian tour. AP Photo

DWIGHT D. EISENHOWER
MONTREAL, CANADA

Queen Elizabeth with US President Dwight D. Eisenhower (1890 - 1969) leaving Lambert Lock, Montreal after taking part in the opening ceremony of the St. Lawrence Seaway, June 26, 1959. Photo by Central Press/Hulton Archive/ Getty Images

JOHN F. KENNEDY
BUCKINGHAM PALACE

June 5, 1961, American President, John F Kennedy, with first lady Jaqueline Kennedy, pictured at Buckingham Palace with Queen Elizabeth II Photo by Popperfoto/Getty Images

RICHARD M. NIXON
WASHINGTON, DC

*American Vice President (and future President)
Richard M. Nixon (1913 - 1994) greets Queen
Elizabeth II of the United Kingdom outside
the US Capitol during her State Visit to
Washington, DC, October 1957.
Photo by Robert Lerner/Getty Images*

JIMMY CARTER
BUCKINGHAM PALACE, LONDON

*President Jimmy Carter with Queen
Elizabeth II at Buckingham Palace London England May 1977, AP Photo*

GEORGE H. W. BUSH
WHITE HOUSE

Queen Elizabeth II waves as she is escorted by Presidnet George H.W. Bush, after the her arrival at the White House on Tuesday, May 14, 1991 in Washington. The Queen is to spend four days in Washington. AP Photo/Doug Mills

WILLIAM J. CLINTON
BUCKINGHAM PALACE

*US President Bill Clinton talks with Elizabeth II along with the First Lady Hillary Rodham Clinton and daughter Chelsea at the Garden Entrance of Buckingham Palace 14 December, 2000 in London, England. The Clintons had tea with the Queen as they were wrapping up their three day trip to Ireland, North Ireland and the UK.
Paul Richards/AFP/Getty Image*

GEORGE W. BUSH, WHITE HOUSE

Queen Elizabeth II and George Bush, President of the USA, deliver speeches at the White House, Washington DC on May 7, 2007. Photo by Anwar Hussein/FilmMagic

BARACK H. OBAMA, BUCKINGHAM PALACE

U.S. President Barack Obama and Queen Elizabeth II during a State Banquet in Buckingham Palace on May 24, 2011 in London, England. The 44th President of the United States, Barack Obama, and his wife Michelle were in the UK for a two day State Visit at the invitation of HM Queen Elizabeth II. During the trip they attended a state banquet at Buckingham Palace and the President addressed both houses of Parliament at Westminster Hall. Photo by Lewis Whyld - WPA Pool/Getty Images

RONALD REAGAN, WINDSOR CASTLE, 1982
Photo by David Hume Kennerly/ Getty Images

Elizabeth, Duchess of York (1900 - 2002), looks at her first child, future Queen, Princess Elizabeth, in May 1926.

Photo by Speaight/Hulton Archive/Getty Images

CHAPTER ONE

Dr. James C. Kelly

WORLD WAR II AND THE QUEEN'S FORMATIVE YEARS

Dr. James Kelly

Elizabeth Alexandra Mary Windsor was born in London on April 21, 1926 to cheers from a crowd gathered outside her parent's house on Bruton Street. The family's dynastic name "Saxe-Coburg-Gotha," acquired when Prince Albert married Queen Victoria, had been changed to the quintessentially English "Windsor" during World War I. Some feared that true monarchy ended when the king of England changed his name, but George V emerged from the war with his throne intact, unlike his Romanov, Hapsburg, and Hohenzollern counterparts. The American president Woodrow Wilson said the "war to end all wars" was fought "to make the world safe for democracy." George V made Britain safe for monarchy. Domestic demand for radical change was channeled into the Labour Party rather than Bolshevism. In 1924, when Labour came to power, George wondered what his grandmother Victoria would have thought of a Labour government, but he showed it every courtesy and was completely above partisanship in his dealings with all parties, a legacy and lesson his great granddaughter would heed and adhere to religiously.

When the writer H. G. Wells accused George V (Elizabeth's grandfather) of heading "an alien and un-inspiring court," he replied that he "might be uninspiring but he'd be damned if he were an alien!" Unlike his father, Edward VII, he cared nothing for Society and was fluent in no language but English, travelling abroad only when forced to in the line of royal duty. He loved country life—Sandringham in Norfolk above all other places—another legacy to his great granddaughter. This was a critical transitional time for European leadership in general and monarchies in particular and he navigated the tricky waters as much through his "ordinariness" as any royal skills learned from his royal predecessors. Twentieth-century Britain needed a figurehead king who represented the whole people but let their elected representatives

speak for them. He was dignified without pomposity and regal without extravagance. Elizabeth knew him as "Grandpa England," and he was an important role model as was his consort, Queen Mary, who owed her position not to wealth or beauty, but to being a great-granddaughter of George III. She still believed that "divinity doth hedge a king," and she set a standard of propriety and duty that her granddaughter in turn emulated.

In 1926, the birth of a daughter to the Duke of York, second-in-line to the throne after his brother Edward, Prince of Wales, was not that newsworthy. The Duke and Duchess of York might well have a son who would immediately displace Elizabeth in the line of accession. The eyes of the world were fixed instead on the dashing heir, the Prince of Wales—"Uncle David" to Elizabeth—who was receiving delirious receptions as he traveled the Empire in the 1920s something for which the Yorks were grateful as it allowed them to go about their lives in relative tranquility.

July 1936: Princess Elizabeth hugging a corgi dog. Photo by Lisa Sheridan/Studio Lisa/Getty Images

By 1935, when Elizabeth rode in the Silver Jubilee procession of King George V and Queen Mary, she had grown in importance. Not only was it increasingly unlikely that she ever would have a brother, but the Prince of Wales—already forty-two years old—seemed disinclined to marry. When a year later he had become King Edward VIII, his choice of a wife was disastrous. His would-be queen was a twice divorced American who was widely viewed as a mere social climber or, to use Queen Mary's vocabulary, "an adventuress." The king was "Defender of the Faith" and the Church of England did not recognize remarriage by divorced persons whose spouses were living. George V and Queen Mary would not even receive divorced people at court. Nor were the dominions inclined to accept such a lady as queen.

In the 1930s the British Empire was the largest it ever had been or would be, but in the year of Elizabeth's birth Great Britain essentially recognized the independence of Canada, Australia, New Zealand, and South Africa. The role of the monarch, thereafter, was to serve as the common bond of the Empire and symbol of its unity. It could not unify around Wallis Simpson or a king who put personal desires ahead of his people.

Elizabeth was kept in ignorance of the crisis until its resolution in December 1936, when Edward VIII abdicated and Elizabeth's father, Prince Albert, succeeded to the throne and took the name George VI.

Princess Elizabeth, age 14, and Princess Margaret Rose (1930 - 2002) on a terrace of the Royal Lodge, Windsor, with gardening equipment and a pet corgi dog in April 1940. Photo by Lisa Sheridan/Studio Lisa/Getty Images

CHAPTER TWO

H. Edward Mann

VIRGINIA AND BRITAIN – THE ENGLISH ANTECEDENTS OF AMERICAN POLITICS AND GOVERNANCE

My visits have "*...given me the opportunity to reaffirm the ideals which we share and the affection that exists between our people -- without which the formalities of alliance would be meaningless, but from the certainty of which our two countries continue to draw strength.*"

"*I visit the United States this week to commemorate the four hundredth anniversary of the landing of a small group of British citizens on a tiny island in what is now called the James River here in Virginia. With the benefit of hindsight, we can see in that event the origins of a singular endeavour, the building of a great nation, founded on the eternal values of democracy and equality based on the rule of law and the promotion of freedom.*"

"*This four hundredth anniversary marks a moment to recognize the deep friendship which exists between our two countries. Friendship is a complex concept. It means being able to debate openly, disagree on occasion, surmount both good times and bad, safe in the knowledge that the bonds that draw us together— of history, understanding and warm regard—are far stronger than any temporary differences of opinion.*"

Her Majesty Queen Elizabeth II, 2007

INTRODUCTION

The British monarchy – and the institutions that grew into that kingdom's current form of government – dates back to 1066 with the reign of William I. Before that time, Britain had been presided over by Romans, Danes, and small English kingdoms, with influences from Celts, Gallic, Normans, Saxons, etc. The role, responsibilities and prerogatives of kings evolved over centuries and were rarely organized in a proactive and strategic fashion. Each king put his own stamp on how he wanted to rule, with the sovereigns gaining more and more power, wealth and control. The authority of monarchs was not effectively challenged until 1215 with the drafting of the Magna Carta, when feudal barons met with King John at Runnymede to place certain checks and balances on his excesses of royal power. This event was an important cornerstone in establishing the concept of the rule of law and contrasted with the prevailing attitude of "might means right."

When the Virginia Company sought to establish business operations in North America in the early 1600's, a completely new and unique set of circumstances awaited them. Although they arrived with British perspectives and prejudices, the New World was more like a blank slate than the continuation of an inevitable process. The three ships (the Susan Constant, Godspeed and Discovery) departed on December 19, 1606. The contrast between the bustling wharves of London and the oasis that greeted them upon arriving on Virginia's shore was more than merely a change in scenery. It was a political opportunity rarely seen on earth.

PRE-1607 –
THE NEW WORLD AS A STATE OF NATURE

Thomas Hobbes: "In such condition there is continual fear, and danger of violent death, and the life of man solitary, poor, nasty, brutish and short."

John Locke: "The state of nature has a law of nature to govern it…" Reason teaches that "…no one ought to harm another in his life, health, liberty, or possessions…"

Mankind "in a state of nature" was, and still is, a political and theoretical device formulated by English political thinkers in the late 1600's to discuss the rights of individuals, as well as how political structures should be devised and limited. It is an oversimplification to put it this way, but Hobbes believed that political structures needed to be developed to keep men from taking advantage of each other. Locke had a more beneficent view of humankind and felt individuals engaged in a social contact with a sovereign or with each other to better themselves by building communities. But both agreed that there are certain rights given to mankind by nature (or by God, depending on one's religious view), and those rights cannot be taken away by monarchies and/or autocratic rulers, the prevailing mode of governance across the planet at the time.

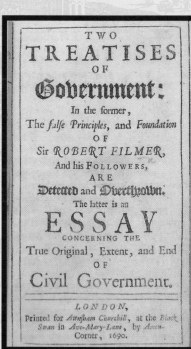

If there ever were an embodiment of the Lockeian state of nature on earth, it was the Chesapeake Bay basin in the years prior to 1607….

The 35,000 Virginia Indians who made up the 3 dozen or so tribes living east of the fall line and west of the Eastern Shore called this land Tsenacomoco and took advantage of an abundant array of flora and fauna for their well-being and sustenance. Written accounts by English explorers shortly after arrival in 1607 talk of a variety of fruits, berries and vegetables seemingly unequaled on earth. They mention that the examples in Virginia seemed bigger, more abundant and decidedly more flavorful. John Smith wrote that on the third day in Virginia he came across:

"...a little plat of ground full of fine and beautiful strawberries, four times bigger and better than ours in England..."

Virginia Indians had a simple agricultural system where corn, beans and chick peas were the plants most regularly cultivated.

This abundance was also evident in the Bay, rivers and creeks of the basin. Bivalves were available in such numbers that oyster beds were actually reefs peeking above the water level at low tide, allowing one to simply row or wade out to the reef and pluck the oysters. Sturgeon at maturity weighed no less than 150 pounds and grew to be 7-10 feet long. In the spring, herring and shad began their spring swim up Virginia rivers - the Powhatan (later called the James), the Pamunkey (later called the York) and the Rappahannock and Potomac. Deer and wild turkeys were readily available, and the agile native hunters became extremely adept at tracking and killing prey for sustenance.

And all of this was done with minimal impact on the land and resources – nature sustained the life of the inhabitants, and she replenished herself. Native Virginians, for their part, had a small impact on their environment, as they were effective and ecofriendly recyclers who left behind a negligible carbon footprint.

Virginia Indians were connected by more than just a common Algonquin language. They also were able to experience a sense of community across a large geographic area due to a federation of tribes under the direction of a supreme chief named Powhatan. His political skill and personal magnetism helped keep order among the various tribes – he minimized their disagreements between each other, while allowing for each of the local communities to more or less govern themselves. Those tribes not included in his confederation were usually handled through alliances - or warfare.

1585 - 1607
THE EARLY CONTACT PERIOD: THE LOST COLONY
AND JAMESTOWN

The first settlers of the Roanoke colony cast off for North America three years before the British defeated the Spanish Armada in 1588. Queen Elizabeth I wanted England to be the master of the seas, as well as to be poised for new markets internationally. This mercantile and pro-business attitude fueled the need for natural resources. Sir Walter Raleigh is credited with the first documented, royally-sanctioned attempt to establish a British colony in North America named Roanoke.

After 5 years and a couple of hundred lives lost, the Roanoke colony failed. The reasons for its collapse and what became of the original settlers – including Virginia Dare, the first English child documented to have been born in North America - have never been firmly established and therefore is destined as The Lost Colony. After the settlement's failure, English authorities and financiers formulated new rules and guidelines, and another attempt was made to establish a commercial outpost on the American east coast. There are some who argue that there were other motives for the establishment of the settlement – they often refer to the propagation of the Christian religion – yet even a casual reading of the Charter of Incorporation for the Virginia Company dated March 1606 reveals the foremost motivation for this effort was a joint stock company. This incorporation is one of the, if not the, first private capital ventures ever established – and it was devised to make money. The early profits were foreseen to be from gold and silver extraction.

When the settlers originally landed in Virginia on April 26, 1607 just south of Cape Henry, they opened a box that had been held under lock and key during the long voyage and read their instructions. The box provided guidance for how the gentlemen and explorers were to rule themselves. A more graphic example of "the rule of law" meets a "state of nature" is hard to find - the instructions named the president and the 7 councilors among the 103 surviving settlers (one had died en route) as well as guidance on how they were to settle disputes.

Among other diverse instructions the settlers were commanded to:

• Travel 100 miles inland before setting up a permanent location – this was done to avoid the possibility of being surprised by an enemy (most likely the Spanish navy).

• Not to offend the "naturals" (natives)

• Don't write back to England with discouraging news

However, the settlers failed to follow some of the more practical advice, such as to avoid settling "… in a low or moist place…" If Jamestown Island were anything, it was low and moist.

1607-1649 GETTING BEYOND MERE SURVIVAL

A manifest of the first settlers/employees and stockholders who offered their sweat equity to the Virginia Company strengthens the argument that the Company was formed as a money-making venture. Included in the first 103 English settlers are perfumers, metallurgists, blacksmiths, carpenters, tailors, etc. Unfortunately this list highlights an incredible naiveté, as there was an assumption there was not much need to import farmers or those involved in the agriculture arts, as food could be easily grown, gathered or traded to Indians for copper trinkets. When hostilities forced the settlers to stay in the fort

(built on the island within a few weeks of their May 13th landing), their food options became limited and over 50% of the English died within 4 months from disease and malnourishment.

Yet even when coming to an uncomfortable understanding with the Indians, and survival looked uncertain at best, members of the Company were still bullish on their prospects, devising ways to take advantage of the natural resources close at hand and make a profit. An abundance of sand suitable for making glass was observed on the riverbank just several hundred yards west of the fort and in 1609 a glassworks was established - the first attempt at manufacturing in America. Additionally, pitch, tar and lumber were added to the list of materials sent back to England – in return, experts in how to organize these industries were brought in from Germany and Poland. This was the beginning of multiculturalism, the concept of America as a melting pot, and the ability of newly arrived-Americans to turn to the rest of the world and recruit (or force) talent and resources from an array of nationalities.

Despite the decision on the part of the Company's business planners to focus on manufacturing, in such a land of limitless natural abundance, it was inevitable that a cash crop would become the first revenue center for the settlement. Economic salvation came to the Virginia Company in 1614 after John Rolfe developed a Virginia-grown strain of sweet smoke from Trinidad favored by the British and shipped four barrels of tobacco to England. After that point there was no stopping the product – from 1616 to 1618 demand for tobacco product increased from 2,300 to 49,528 pounds, and by 1628 had reached a total of a half a million pounds exported per year.

John Rolfe, for his role in recognizing a business opportunity and developing a plan for distribution and marketing, is considered by many to be the first entrepreneur in America. He is much better known for having married Pocahontas, the daughter of Powhatan. This was not an inconsequential move in and of itself, for it helped to diffuse tension between the English newcomers and the native Virginians for several years.

During this period, and after some experimentation in martial law, private land ownership in Virginia became a reality, with incentives to long-time settlers, newly arrived explorers, shareholders in the Virginia Company and to anyone who paid the cost of passage for new colonists. This contrasted with the feudal practices in England where most agricultural efforts were sustained by individuals who were tenant farmers for life.

As the struggling effort began to slowly succeed, increased population, land acquisition, success in trade, etc., again called into question how to best govern the settlement. On Friday, July 30th 1619, the first representative government in North America met in the church at Jamestown, as 22 members from 11 districts met in the sweltering Virginia summer. The legislative model for representative government was based on British practices and tradition – oath taking and checking credentials, the presence of a Clerk to document, deliberations, the formats for debate, etc. The elected members (called Burgesses) of the General Assembly met together with the Governor and other appointed officials

in a general court to make decisions. For decades the annual or semi-annual meetings of the Assembly were considered a little parliament in Virginia, yet that first session adjourned after only 5 days due to the "extreme heat." In fact, one member died - possibly of heat stroke - during their deliberations.

That same year – 1619 – a ship named the White Lion containing 20 or so Africans arrived in Virginia. On the surface the human cargo addressed an important and immediate concern for the settlement – workers were needed for the labor-intensive demands of planting, growing, reaping, curing and shipping tobacco. Originally treated as indentured servants - workers hired for a set time (usually 7 years) and then given their freedom - the rights of this class of worker were gradually forgotten within the next decade or so. In 1625 there were 25 slaves in Virginia. 25 years later, there were 300 and in 1671 there were 2,000, accounting for about five percent of the population. In 1662 a Virginia statute stated that Africans were no longer to be treated as indentured servants but were in service for life. The codification of the slave laws after this date began the spread of the biggest stain on 17th and 18th century Anglo-American experiments in individual liberty. What cannot be overlooked is how three ethnic and racial groups – 1) English and West Europeans, 2) Virginia Indians and 3) Africans – interrelated and interacted, positively and negatively, with various laws, customs and practices melded together to shape and evolve into a distinctly Virginian and American culture.

1649-1776 EXPERIMENTS IN SELF-GOVERNMENT

In May 1625, Virginia was transformed from a Company to a royal dominion and crown colony. Yet Virginia's very existence was challenged in 1622 and in 1644 by Indian uprisings. A less graphic, yet more long-term challenge was how to overcome the obstacles presented by the huge distances and time required to receive answers from authorities in London. Life went on - decisions on many matters had to be dealt with locally, and the government's representatives were forced to make expedient choices without guidance from England. In 1649 a completely new and baffling challenge arose – to whom should such questions be addressed? King Charles the First had been beheaded and, as the leadership of Virginia was decidedly royalist, it would not do to ask the dreaded Roundheads (followers of Cromwell) for advice. Therefore practical expedience seeped into the consciousness of authorities in Virginia, and maybe the people themselves, to realize they could govern their own land without edicts from a monarch 3000 miles away.

In 1676 the sovereignty of the people - and who best represented it - manifested itself in a way that no one could foresee. It grew out of what was primarily a personality conflict between the Royal Governor-General Sir William Berkeley (a friend of Charles the First) and a quick-tempered young plantation owner named Nathaniel Bacon. When Bacon became dissatisfied with the Governor-General Berkeley for his lack of response in protecting frontier settlers from Indian incursions – the frontier being defined as settlements 50 miles from Jamestown – he took it upon himself to mobilize a militia. After successfully pushing the Indians back, Bacon then turned his sights on the Governor-General. In a series of dramatic confrontations over several months, he ultimately set fire to Jamestown and led America's first political insurrection of armed Englishmen. In the middle of battling for leadership of the colony, he suddenly died of dysentery and his followers disbanded. Whether his actions were justified is still controversial three hundred years after the event, but the fact cannot be lost that just several years prior to this American revolt, it was the English citizenry who in 1649 had first checked executive authority of the British government - by chopping off the head of King Charles the First. This instance and Bacon's actions probably caused many Virginia leaders to look over their own shoulder (and rub their neck) when groups of angry citizens assembled.

Despite these events, the business of Virginia began to prosper, with some luck and much hard labor. This labor - much of it built on the backs of African slaves - led to a rise with all the attending benefits to life in the middle class. Although they could afford to do it, white Virginians began to tire of having to send their sons all the way to Harvard or England for an education and it was time to demand a school of their own. In 1693 King William and Queen Mary chartered the College of William and Mary in Virginia at Middle Plantation later named Williamsburg. The Rev. James Blair spent several years appealing to the Royal Court to adopt the College's charter – and then 50 years serving as the College's first President.

Upon reflection, the idea of keeping the college's name (after the 1776 break with England) is not far-fetched when one realizes their joint reign – 1689 -1702 - was a huge step towards establishing the rule of law for the average Englishman. A mere 90 years prior, King James, for whom Jamestown was named, had written a document expressing his firm belief in the divine right of kings. In 1689, the "Glorious Revolution" brought King William of Orange (a Dutch prince) and his wife Queen Mary (daughter of James II) to the British throne as co-regents. This action was accompanied by Parliament issuing a Declaration of Rights, limiting royal prerogatives and establishing the primacy of Parliament. This document bans the king from dissolving parliament, prevents the sovereign from raising taxes without agreement from parliament, assures the freedom of speech and the right to bear arms.

As previously mentioned, the Slave Code in Virginia set into law those practices that had been informally followed for years. Great Britain was not exempt from this system of exploitation as well. Even as abolitionist efforts were more vocal in England, the country's political leadership conveniently looked the other way due to the money and wealth the "peculiar institution" brought to the Empire.

After 1700, Britain was willing to invest in America – but it increasingly turned to the colonies to pay its own way. Taxes were levied on America by the British Parliament to fund the debts incurred by the French and Indian war (or what the British called the "Seven Years' War"). This led to a series of remarkable blunders made by both Parliament and King George the Third, including the "Intolerable Act," the Townsend Act, The Stamp Act, The Tea Act, The Quartering Act, etc. What the King and his government did not appreciate was the rise of the American nation, and it is difficult to separate how much of what occurred in 1776 was due to 1) their mistakes or 2) the inevitable rise of a people who began to gain a sense of themselves as a unique community separated from their English brothers and sisters by more than just distance.

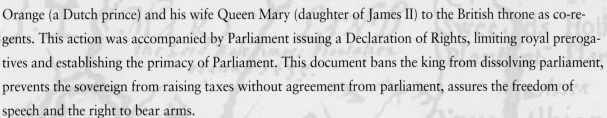

1776 and Beyond

Experiments in democracy - or reliance on an understanding of British political antecedents, for that matter - did not end in 1776 with the Declaration of Independence. In fact, the next 12 years proved to be an intense tutorial on how to structure liberty and the states served as 13 incubators or laboratories on how to best achieve the hopes of liberty.

The end of the American War of Independence in 1781 was not the final word on whether the American experiment would survive. Political and diplomatic relationships between Britain and the United States did not begin on a strong foundation, and Great Britain kept a wary eye on their former colony. Trade and diplomatic tensions resulted in a second war (The War of 1812) which was settled by the Treaty of Ghent in 1814. Unfortunately America spent much time, many resources and far too much intellectual capital afterwards on the domestic issue of slavery. England took the first steps in the world to outlaw slavery by passing the Slave Trade Act of 1807 and outlawed slavery outright in the Slavery Abolition Act of 1833.

In America, friction between the North and the pro-slavery South grew, and sectional primacy came at the expense of national unity. British observers who visited America included Charles Dickens in 1842, who noted in his book *American Notes* his personal disgust with slavery. Unfortunately events were proving that an area where the US Constitution fell short was in addressing slavery, an issue that festered on the American political scene for another 80 years.

With the outbreak of the War Between the States, the British government initially adopted a wait-and-see attitude. While a strong business relationship was built with southern cotton being exported to its mills in England, many English leaders and citizens were also emotionally supportive of the abolitionist tendencies of the Republican Party and the Lincoln administration.

Contrasted with Great Britain's leadership in the Industrial Revolution during the last half of the 19th century, this period was not a time when Virginia or the American South was known for economic dynamism. Financially, it was near impossible to find the revenue to repair the destruction of the war (over 45% of the battles in the war took place on Virginia soil). The toll was not just on the infrastructure, roads, bridges, ports, and trains, etc., but also led to substantial drain on financial and human capital as well – an entire generation of young men was decimated. Opportunities - the emergence of exports such

"Visit of the Prince of Wales, President Buchanon and Dignataries to the tomb of Washington at Mt. Vernon, October 1860" by Thomas P. Rossiter. Smithsonian American Art Museum

as coal and the reemergence of tobacco (due to the manufacturing process for rolling cigarettes) were only a couple of bright spots in the decade's long reversal of fortunes for the South. With the exception of the emotional salve provided by the romantic ideals inherent in The Lost Cause, the nadir of Virginia and the south was apparent to most outsiders - even if many Virginians did what they could to avoid thinking about it.

THE 20TH CENTURY
FIGHTING FOR, AND CELEBRATING, DEMOCRACY IN A NEW CENTURY

In both 1807 and 1857, there had been commemorative events on Jamestown Island consisting primarily of military reviews and speeches. At the turn of the 20th century, local planners saw the 300th not only as an opportunity for economic growth, but also an opportunity to re-live the glory days of Virginia's pre-eminence and political leadership. 1907 was in the era of world's fairs – and Norfolk, as a transportation hub merely 50 miles via the James River from Jamestown, and, most importantly, with hard-to-come-by money for investment, lent itself to funding a bigger, more expansive event than did the original site. Land was bought, plans were developed and an infrastructure was built for access to Sewell's Point as the site of the commemoration.

President Theodore Roosevelt (fourth from right) arrives at Jamestown Exposition, April 26, 1907.

Known as the "Jamestown Exhibition," the event was held from April – December 1907 and had over three million visitors, including Theodore Roosevelt, Mark Twain, Booker T. Washington, Kaiser Wilhelm and others. A significant foreign policy opportunity came about when in December 1907 President Roosevelt launched a flotilla of 16 battleships - nicknamed the Great White Fleet – on a 14-month round-the-world cruise to establish America as a key player in world affairs. This cruise was not a direct challenge to British superiority of the seas, but it did show the rest of the globe that the United States was certainly in the same league. Within a decade, the combined British American armada was called upon to match the German Navy in World War I. The effectiveness of allied navies was given an operational enhancement in 1917 when the US Navy bought and converted the former site of the Jamestown Exhibition into the Norfolk Naval Base, now the largest naval base in the world.

Improvements in transatlantic transportation allowed leaders from countries to visit each other, and the first state visit to America by a reigning British monarch came in 1939 when King George VI visited the United States.

King George VI and his wife Queen Elizabeth (parents of Princess Elizabeth, the future Queen Elizabeth II) survey the damage to Buckingham Palace after it was bombed by German aircraft in a raid over London September 13 1940. @BBC

"In 1939, my father was the first reigning British sovereign to visit America, and he and President Roosevelt talked long and earnestly about the coming crisis. At the end of their visit, Mrs. Roosevelt wrote that "in time of danger," as she put it, "something deeper comes to the surface and the British and we stand firmly together with confidence in our common heritage and ideas." - Queen Elizabeth II

HER MAJESTY QUEEN ELIZABETH II

Two years later, after American entry into World War II, Prime Minister Winston Churchill and President Franklin Roosevelt crisscrossed the Atlantic numerous times for face to face discussions – in fact, Churchill was in Washington meeting with Roosevelt at the White House just a few days after Pearl Harbor.

The Nazi air attacks on London led to a response by the English people that Churchill called "their finest hour.' Despite massive bombing of the metropolitan area, British citizens maintained their businesses, families and daily routines as much as possible. The Royal family stepped up as well. Rather than retreat to the outskirts of London to avoid the bombings, George VI and his wife stayed in London, sharing deprivations with the people, even though Buckingham Palace took direct hits. The future Queen, Princess Elizabeth, showed her mettle by serving in the Women's Auxiliary Territorial Service as a mechanic and military truck driver, rising to the rank of honorary junior commander.

After the war, the close bonds between Great Britain and Virginia were strengthened and celebrated. On March 8, 1946, accompanied by Supreme Allied Commander General Dwight D. Eisenhower, former British Prime Minister Winston Churchill was greeted by 30,000 citizens lining the streets of Richmond as he made his way to the Virginia State Capitol to deliver a speech before a joint session of the General Assembly. Later that same afternoon he made a pilgrimage to the College of William and Mary and also visited Colonial Williamsburg.

The strain of being a war-time monarch took its toll on King George VI and he died in February 1952 at the age of 56. In 1952, Queen Elizabeth at the age of 31 became the second British monarch to visit America when she came to commemorate the 350-year anniversary of Jamestown in October 1957.

Her Majesty Queen Elizabeth was trained as a mechanic serving in the British Auxiliary Territorial Service during World War II. Photo courtesy of the Camera Press.

Former British Prime Minister Churchill speaks before a joint session of the Virginia General Assembly in the Hall of the House of Delegates on March 8, 1946. Photo by Frank Dementi.

Although it was hoped this event would help to revive Virginia's global reputation, the Queen arrived in Virginia in the midst of a domestic political storm. U.S. Senator Harry F. Byrd, the most influential political leader in Virginia, urged the white citizens of the Commonwealth not to comply with the 1954 Brown vs. Board of Education decision from the U.S. Supreme Court. This decision stated that separate school systems were inherently unequal and violated the intention of the 14th Amendment. In what was labeled as "Massive Resistance," opposition to the decision included de-funding and closing school systems that integrated. It was the prevailing attitude of the political leadership in Virginia until a final federal court case in January 1959 declared the schools must open.

Though this final court decision came 15 months after the Queen's visit, in 1957, Virginians rolled out the red carpet, put their best foot forward and took a small break from fractious events to commemorate what had been achieved in the previous 350 years.

CHAPTER THREE

The Lord Watson
of Richmond, CBE

THE QUEEN, ENGLISH AND THE SPREAD OF DEMOCRACY

On May 3rd 2007 I was in the Virginia State Capitol to hear a speech delivered by Her Majesty The Queen. Earlier that day she had flown into Richmond from London accompanied by His Royal Highness Prince Philip. The occasion was the 400th Anniversary of the arrival of three small ships from England, the Godspeed, the Susan Constant and the Discovery in 1607. The Queen had this to say about the significance of that event:

"With the benefit of hindsight we can see in that event the origins of a singular endeavour, the building of a great nation, founded on the eternal values of democracy and equality based on the rule of law and the promotion of freedom."

I was present in the State Capitol because for the previous two years I had co-chaired the British Jamestown Committee which had helped to organise the celebration of the 400th Anniversary on both sides of the Atlantic.

Richmond, Virginia and Richmond-upon-Thames are sister cities and it had been on my first visit to Richmond that I had been taken to the James River and seen the site of that first settle-

Richmond England (above) and Richmond Virginia (below)
Legend has it that in 1737 William Byrd named the city of Richmond Virginia after Richmond upon Thames (20 miles upriver from London). He remembered from his youth the remarkable similarities in the topography and views of their respective rivers.

Photo: Tonya Rice

Her Majesty, Queen Elizabeth II, begins her first remarks for this state visit with an address to a joint session of the Virginia General Assembly in the newly renovated Capitol on May 3, 2007 (also pictured: Virginia House of Delegates Speaker William J. Howell (left) and Lieutenant Governor William T. Bolling

ment. I became fascinated by it and its significance for Britain, America and now the world. Essentially Jamestown marks the start of the voyage of English – a journey which has taken the language to its present role as the working language of the global village used by more than two billion people. But this would not and could not have happened without the world shaping success of the other elements of the intellectual property brought by the settlers - a notion of free enterprise, a concept of law and an instinct for freedom.

The truth was that those who crossed in the *Susan Constant*, the *Godspeed* and the *Discovery* could have no concept of the value of their cargo. Much more potent than their seeds, their guns and their gunpowder was their intellectual property – the ideas and concepts that would come to shape the modern world and the United States. Notions of representative government, the rule of law and capitalism travelled in the heads of settlers, not in the holds of their ships. But, most important of all, these ideas were expressed in English – a language at a unique point in its development with the inherent flexibility and creativity to adapt to and then itself mould the New World.

The voyage of English and the drivers that have made it the world's working language need to be understood. They explain – in great part – how we have arrived where we now are, living in a globalised interdependent world. These drivers stem from those first transported across the Atlantic as the intellectual property of the settlers, all expressed in the English language. Later their ideas would ride with great movements of people. They would be spread by the British Diaspora, and they would be part of the process that transformed the millions who passed through Ellis Island to become Americans. These same values drove the development of the United States. In two World Wars and in the Cold War, they were challenged and might have succumbed. They are tested today by Muslim extremism. Yet the confluence of English and globalisation creates a flood of such force it is hard to envisage how it could be halted, let alone reversed.

The language itself and its unique flowering at the time of the settlers is thus where the story begins. John Milton's nephew, writing about this flowering of English a century later, described it as *The New World of English Words*. Up to 12,000 new words were added to the language during the Elizabethan age. No one would deploy them with greater effect than William Shakespeare.

His last play, *The Tempest*, which drew on Sir Walter Ralegh's experiences and Bartholomew Gosnold's geography, came out in 1611, the same year as the publication of the King James Bible. This was indeed the flowering of the English language. The authors of *The Story of English* sum up Shakespeare's gift to English in this way: "Shakespeare put the vernacular to work and showed those who came after what could be done with it. He filled a universe with words."

And what a universe! There were his panoplies of English history but also of everyone else's, from ancient Rome to the Plantagenets, from Malta to Denmark and peopled by unforgettable men and women struggling with every emotion and with fate: Hamlet, Macbeth, Caesar, King Lear – an army of tyrants and heroes relieved by comic and elemental characters like Falstaff. Here indeed was the vernacular used as never before: the accents of Irish, Welsh and Scots in the King's service as well as the language of the Court; King's men and Kings, courtiers and common folk. Yet the English Language even impelled forward by the creative explosion of Shakespeare's genius would not have transformed the world if it had

The Commonwealth of Virginia's fleet—replicas of the Discovery, Susan Constant, and Godspeed—sail down the James marking the 400th anniversary of the settlers' first landing at Cape Henry on April 26, 2007. Courtesy of the Jamestown Yorktown Foundation

had not been for the potency of the rest of the intellectual property carried by the first colonists. Part of this remarkable confluence was Capitalism.

The colonists had plentiful backers. One was Sir Thomas Smythe who had an interest in the Royal Patent for all produce from America previously held by Sir Walter Ralegh. Sir Thomas won the support of James the First to grant a Charter to the first Virginia Company. Two years after the colonists had precariously secured a base on the James and called it Jamestown, King James attended a banquet in the Great Hall in Guildhall to celebrate his charter. More than 50 Livery Companies and London's Lord Mayor joined in the venture.

The colony's economic vitality was ultimately secured by the tobacco introduced by John Rolfe. But tobacco came too late to save the company itself which folded in 1624. The joint stock company gave way to direct rule by the Crown. This, however, brought to centre stage the other potent dimension of the colony's DNA.

From the rediscovered James Fort, the monumental Captain John Smith peers at the end of a summer day over the palisade and into the James River, where ships bearing English settlers and supplies arrived four centuries earlier. Photo courtesy of the National Park Service.

There was another notion in the minds of the first English colonists which would prove equally decisive. It had to do with the rule of law and government. Without the eventual but overwhelming success of these concepts in the English-speaking world and their effective defence in two World Wars and in the Cold War the fate of the language would have been quite different.

The first tests came early both in the New World and the Old. Patrick Wormald, the late author of *The Making of English Law*, gave a memorable lecture at Canterbury in 2003 – his theme being Ethelbert's code of law. In it he asserted: "English language and law are the most enduring marks of Englishness, its main claims to anyone else's attention." There are many tributaries to the river of English law but its flow has shaped the contours of constitutional development on both sides of the Atlantic and in remarkably similar ways.

The first General Assembly convened in 1619, and represented the interests of those who had them – even then – to defend. Indentured servants, women and, in due course, slaves would play no part. The House of Burgesses was there for the gentry and although a Crown Colony, Virginia was really ruled by its assembly and in an epoch when all the colonial assemblies were rising in power and vigour it had no rival for self assertiveness.

Asserting their rights would lead the colonial assemblies along the path to independence from the English Crown as inevitably as the assertion of the rights of Parliament led the House of Commons to rebellion against Charles I. As Cromwell and the largely East Anglian land-owning gentry made plain in the Putney Debates following the Civil War, they were quite clear that victory against the King should not open the way for the Levellers. But later the Levellers would win and democracy take over the institutions of law-making with the symbolic cooperation of the Monarchy. This was the English, and then British, political evolution.

In America, rebellion against the Crown could not be followed by a restoration. There would be no American successor to George III and he knew it. After overcoming his own anger he even sought to put a good face on it. In a letter after the Peace of Paris had been signed in September 1783 he wrote of the outcome and the Americans: "I cannot conclude without mentioning how sensibly I feel the dismemberment of America from this Empire and that I should be miserable indeed if I did not feel that no blame on that account can be laid at my door, and did I not also know that knavery seems to be so much the striking feature of its inhabitants that it may not in the end by an evil that they become Alien to this Kingdom!"

Yet, the Declaration of Independence marks a high point in the harnessing of English to political expression. Its words and phrases still ring with relevance. "Life, liberty and the pursuit of happiness" has never been bettered as the justification of the state and the object of politics. Its authors were not fully alert to its implications and could not know its consequences. Another American history puts it well: "Jefferson's doctrine that all men are created equal ... gradually came to mean that all men are equal ... although Jefferson did not mean to include slaves as men, public opinion finally came to regard slaves as inconsistent with the Declaration".

A dinner held March 20 2006 in the ancient Guildhall in the City of London. The dinner, held by British and American commemoration leadership, was in honor of the 400th anniversary of the incorporation of the Virginia Company and was on the spot where in 1609 King James dined and was briefed on the Virginia Charter. @British Jamestown Committee

Yet, if the Virginian formula was self-contradictory and the Declaration of Independence unintended in its consequences, both emanated from the English sense of the law and were expressed in the English language. The United States was without precedent but not without antecedents!

"Independence meant sailing forth on an uncharted sea", wrote American historians Samuel Eliot Morison and Henry Steele Commager in *The Growth of the American Republic,* but "all the mystic chords of memory which (as Abraham Lincoln said) make a people a nation responded in 1775 to English names and events – Magna Carta, Sir Francis Drake, Queen Elizabeth, the Glorious Revolution, the Bill of Rights."

No wonder, then, that the Continental Congresses assumed English as the language of the new United States. Indeed, John Adams, one of its most powerful participants, was the language's most eloquent advocate. His reasons were patriotic: English would facilitate the rise of America and promote her influence around the world. Adams saw the destiny of the new United States as a continental power. A whole continent was its "proper domain" for as he put it: "From the time we became an independent nation it was as much a law of nature that this would become our claim that the Mississippi should flow to the sea."

He was convinced that English would become "more generally the language of the world than Latin was or French is in the present age." Why? In his view it was obvious that America's growing population, its intercourse with other nations and the continuing world role of Great Britain would all combine to "force their language into general use." It would become "the most universally read and spoken" language in the world, to the great benefit of the United States.

So it has proved, with English today ranked with Hindi, Chinese and Arabic as amongst the world's most numerous languages but uniquely because of the number of people using it as an adopted second language rather than as their native tongue. The reasons for this are numerous and many are contemporary such as the internet but the global embrace of English as the key shared language depends critically on the events and outcomes of the nineteenth and twentieth centuries.

The great diaspora of English Speaking peoples from Great Britain to the Empire and to the USA like the tide of non-English Speaking Peoples which was to flow into the United States as immigrants, could only occur with the abolition of slavery both in the British Empire and in the USA.

Freedom was the vital precondition for both these movements of millions – those leaving English ports and those passing through the eye of the needle at Ellis Island into America. These great waves of emigration and immigration ultimately provided the manpower and manufacturing that enabled the Allies to win World War I and to deny both Hitler and Stalin the defeat of Democracy. So the abolition of slavery was decisive.

Before either the British Diaspora or the American "melting pot" could achieve world-changing scale political developments springing from *habeas corpus* and experience in the English language were to transform both the British Empire and the United States. Both had to abolish slavery. Both had become significantly dependent on it. For both, slavery's abolition became a precondition of ultimate self respect.

Britain initiated both the trade in slaves between West Africa and America's East Coast and its abolition, but the history of the trade offers no moral high ground. A series of tests in Eng-

lish courts rendered the ownership of a slave onshore in England illegal, but many Englishmen profited enormously from the trade. Sir John Hawkyns, in three voyages between 1562 and 1568, mapped the logistics and established the economic viability of the trade. The initial focus was the supply of slaves to the West Indies and to Spanish as well as English owners. The African Company was formed in 1562 and the first three hundred Negro slaves taken from Sierra Leone were sold for a spectacular profit in San Domingo. From then on the lucrative triangular route proved an irresistible investment – goods to trade for slaves from Bristol or Liverpool to Africa's West Coast; slaves brutally packed below decks from the Coast to the West Indies or increasingly Virginia; the return to England laden with sugar or tobacco or, by the outbreak of the American Civil War, mainly cotton.

The economic interests involved became enormous. Bristol and Liverpool prospered and became grand. In the West Country, mansions rose for the absentee landlords whose wealth depended on the sugar plantations of Jamaica and the Islands. In London clubs aristocrats would gamble their estates and the slaves working them, lives determined by the fall of the dice and thousands of miles away made nightmarish by the fall of the lash. As abolition was to demonstrate, the sugar economy of the British Empire was dependent on cheap and brutalised labour.

In the US the economics of slavery seemed even more irresistible. Starting as a trade tied to the introduction of tobacco by John Rolfe in 1619, by Independence one in five Americans was black. At Independence the seven Northern States abolished the institution although many of the traders were New England merchants. But as the Union expanded, Northern and the slave owning Southern states progressed in parallel and by 1819 they balanced each other. This precarious see-saw between slave and free was maintained by a series of compromises – thus Missouri's admission as a slave state in 1821 was balanced by Maine's admission as a free state. But a momentum for slavery was building and its driver was cotton. "King Cotton" overtook sugar and tobacco as the key cash crop and England's Industrial Revolution was the cause. The mills of Lancashire became insatiable. By the time of the American Civil War Europe, and especially England, was taking 90 per cent of its cotton from the Southern States and these exports accounted for half the Union's total.

The abolition of the trade in the British Empire and of slavery itself in the Union thus had to overcome very powerful economic interests. How this was achieved differed dramatically – a series of Acts of Parliament in England, a civil war in America. Yet in both cases the arguments for abolition would be based on principle and conscience, fired by non-conformist passion and expressed by writing and rhetoric which enhanced the language, drawing on the heritage of the law and the promise of representative government and contributing decisively to the political future of the English-speaking peoples.

Abolishing the slave trade in the Empire did not lead rapidly or easily to emancipation in the colonies. Achieving both required not only moral righteousness but the command of the seas and command of a majority in Parliament. The Society for the Abolition of the Slave Trade was set up in 1787 by the evangelicals of the Clapham Sect and the Quakers. Prominent in Clapham, where many of them lived as neighbours, was William Wilberforce. His brother-in-law James Stephen had practiced law in the West Indies and from the start the abolitionists focused on the legal barriers to abolition and how best

to dismantle them. Stephen's son was to pursue the task till ultimate victory in 1834 when, on August 1st, all slaves in the Empire became free. Infused with all the romance of Liberal Imperialism, the historian G. M. Trevelyan has written of that moment: "On the last night of slavery the Negroes in our West Indian Islands went up to the hill tops to watch the sun rise, bringing them freedom as its first rays struck the waters."

But for this to happen the British had to have an Empire on which the sun never set! The utter defeat of France in 1815 enabled Britain to act alone and enforce its will. The Royal Navy was the ultimate instrument of abolition. By 1836 James Stephen Jr. had become Permanent Under-Secretary at the Colonial Office and that Office ensured the Navy fulfilled the will of Parliament. It was the fall of Wellington's government and the passing of the Great Reform Bill of 1832 that had created the parliamentary majority needed for abolition – command of a majority and command of the seas did for slavery! The reformers of the time were exhilarated. They *"felt they were at the beginning of a new age when political action could alter the course of history."*

Empowerment and the heady ability to "alter the course of history" proved far harder for the abolitionist cause in the United States although, as in Britain, its ultimate achievement was through the legislature. In 1865 Congress passed the necessary Constitutional Amendment that *"Neither slavery nor involuntary servitude shall exist within the United States."* The contradiction between liberty based on habeas corpus and slavery evident in the Virginian Assembly and manifest in the Declaration of Independence was thus finally resolved, but only after a civil war in which 618,000 Americans were killed and 400,000 wounded.

Such tragedy and such high stakes have engendered some of the finest passages in the English language. It was to happen in 1940 in the speeches of Winston Churchill. It happened in 1863 at the site of one of the bloodiest battles of the Civil War. The language of Lincoln's Gettysburg Address, like Churchill's before and during the Battle of Britain, welds together present anguish with future purpose. It is the rhetoric of democracy at its most sublime:

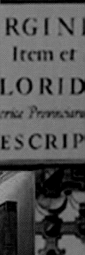

"Fourscore and seven years ago our fathers brought forth upon this continent a new nation, conceived in liberty and dedicated to the proposition that all men are created equal. Now we are engaged in a great civil war, testing whether that nation ... so conceived and so dedicated can long endure ... we cannot hallow this ground. The brave men, living and dead who struggled here have consecrated it far above our power to act or detract. It is rather ... that we here highly resolved that the dead shall not have died in vain, that this nation under God shall have a new birth of freedom and that government of the people, by the people and for the people shall not perish from the earth."

Freedom was the most important single issue tested and settled by the titanic struggles of the centuries that followed the abolition of slavery. However, injustice and inequality distorted and marred the freedom won over slavery and a long and painful struggle ensued in both the US and UK to protect diversity. As The Queen expressed it at the Virginia State Capital that May afternoon in 2007.

"Fifty years on we are now in a position to reflect more candidly on the Jamestown Legacy. Human progress rarely occurs without cost. And these early years when three great civilizations came together for the first time – Western European, Native American and African – released a train of events which continues to have a profound social impact, not only in the US but also in the UK and Europe. Over the course of my reign my country has become a much more diverse society, just as the Commonwealth of Virginia and the whole of the USA have also undergone major social change."

It is to the great credit of both the USA and the UK that these changes have been pursued and achieved within the democratic framework. Change has been constitutional.

In 1991 Her Majesty the Queen addressed the US Congress. She said this:

"A significant part of your social contract is written down in your Constitution. Ours rest on custom and will. The spirit behind both, however, is precisely the same. It is in the spirit of democracy."

The truth, nevertheless, is that constitutional democracy, however enshrined would have shrivelled or been snuffed out if the UK and the US had been defeated by the tyrannies of the Twentieth Century. There would have been no Diamond Jubilee to celebrate, no shared values in which to rejoice, and English would not be the global language it is today.

Both World Wars and the Cold War imperilled the rise and reach of English as well as the peoples speaking the language. Defeat in any of the three conflicts would have constricted, perhaps terminated, the expansion in its use. In the most extreme case, victory for the Third Reich and a Nazi occupation of the British Isles, the language might have so declined that eventually its continuance could have been in doubt. The Nazis expected Russian and Polish to disappear as advanced languages. A form of pidgin German would have been enough to ensure orders were obeyed. Compulsory illiteracy – for *untermenschen* were not entitled to education – in the end would put paid to the Slavic languages.

In the event, the DNA of the Jamestown settlement, the intellectual property transported to the New World in 1607, proved too potent for the assailants of the English-speaking world. Quite specifically, the concepts of law and individual freedom provided the values of the English-speaking allies in all three contests. Free enterprise and capitalism provided the wherewithal for victory. The language knitted together the alliance and gave expression to its purposes. The New World and the British Diaspora returned to address the balance of the Old. The Nineteenth Century did determine the outcome of the Twentieth. Bismarck was right.

The contribution of both the Empire and the United States was decisive in World War I. Germany was halted by France but France was so maimed that her soldiers mutinied in 1917. She could not have defeated Wilhelm's armies. Petain, as "Saviour of Verdun," knew it only too well and in 1940 he was ready to surrender to Hitler's Wehrmacht. Britain was able to keep France in World War I by taking the main impact of the enemy on the Somme, at Paschendale and during Ludendorf's offensives in 1918. But could Britain have won without the contribution of the Empire throughout and the intervention – potential and actual - of the United States at the end? It is unlikely and it seemed so at the time. Speaking at a "Liberty Day" meeting held in Central Hall, Westminster, on July 4th 1918 Winston Churchill found exactly the right words: "A million American soldiers have arrived on the continent of Europe (cheers) and in the nick of time (cheers)."

As for the Empire the statistical evidence is startling. In all, ten million men enlisted under the British flag in World War I; of these 3,284,743 came from the overseas Empire. Of the 947,023 killed, 202,321 were from the Empire. There were nine colonial divisions on the Western Front alone.

The considered judgement of the historian Avner Offer, in the Oxford History of the British Empire published exactly 80 years after the end of the conflict, is worth considering for the perspective it brings: Some of the best assets of British security turned out to be the bonds of the English speaking world overseas: economic, social, political, sentimental, forming a complex but effective system of practice kinship... The military effort of the Dominions was formidable. Canada, Australia and New Zealand mobilized 1.2 million men. India another million.

If economic power, bravery and military and naval punch all played their part, so too – and crucially – did the language. The British overseas and the Americans, whether of British origin or assimilated into the United States by language, responded to the same linked values. During his speech at Central Hall in 1918 Churchill claimed "a great harmony" between the "spirit and language of the Declaration of Independence and all that we are fighting for now." He explained that the Declaration was not only an American document: "It followed on Magna Carta and the Bill of Rights as the third great title deed on which the liberties of the English speaking people are founded." He saw the war as one between nations "where peoples own Governments and nations where the Governments own peoples." And, puzzlingly perhaps for his audience, he insisted that after Germany had been crushed "The Declaration of Independence and all that it implies must cover them too."

That certainly was the view of Woodrow Wilson across the Atlantic. Addressing Congress on America's declaration of war on the German Empire – with the German people he had no quarrel – his message was identical to Churchill's: "We shall fight for the things which we have always carried nearest to our hearts – for Democracy, for the right of those who submit to authority to have a voice in their own Governments." America's aim was "to make the world itself at last free."

World War II was the Twentieth Century's most direct and unrestrained attack on intellectual rights and the freedom of nations. For Hitler the Anglo-Saxon powers, Britain and the United States, were not the only nor the primary targets. The Soviet Union was always his principle objective, its utter conquest the means of achieving Lebensraum for Germany forever and a thousand year Reich from the Rhine to

the Volga. The other focus for his fury – the Jews – became his victims and he their murderer-in-chief wherever the Nazis held sway. Had the Nazis occupied the British Isles their fate would have been sealed. The Isle of Wight was earmarked as a possible British Auschwitz.

Yet if Britain and America were not Hitler's main enemies, their defeat was the precondition for a thousand year Reich. In particular, Britain's resistance in 1940 proved the tipping point. When Hitler called off the invasion project – Operation Sealion – he set in train two consequences which led to his defeat. He invaded Russia with Britain still in the war. Britain thus became the base from which an Anglo-American invasion could and would be launched and from where the British and US air forces would devastate Germany's cities and distort and dislocate her military resources. He also faced a war on two fronts which, if avoided, might well have given him ultimate victory in Russia or long delayed the USSR's revenge. And if, after unimaginable slaughter, the Russians had prevailed and occupied Germany it is unlikely that they would have stopped there. With no Anglo-American armies in Western Europe Stalin could have occupied the entire continent. As the most comprehensive historian of *The Battle of Britain*, Stephen Bungay, puts it: "If Britain had given up in 1940 the war could have had one of two possible outcomes: Nazi or Soviet domination of Europe."

That Britain did not give up was due in large part to Winston Churchill. He steadied the country's nerve, bolstered its courage and rendered negotiations with Hitler unimaginable. He achieved all this by force of will, energy, ability, self-confidence and the utter conviction that the fate of a free world would turn on British defiance. He felt that all his life had been a preparation for this moment. He walked with destiny, yet it is hard to see how he could have achieved success without his command of the English language. Indeed, he had spent a lifetime mastering the language. Now, in 1940, he "mobilized it and sent it into battle." Whoever originated that phrase, Churchill's own sums up what happened: "If I found the right words, you must remember that I have always earned my living by my pen and by my tongue. It was the nation and a race dwelling all around the globe that had the lion heart. I had the luck to be called upon to give the roar."

So, in World War II, as in World War I, the New World had to come to the rescue of the Old. This time the Americans came earlier and in greater numbers. This time they incurred far more casualties and this time they ended up in Berlin, although Eisenhower's caution while saving lives ensured that they arrived in the former Reich capital only with Soviet agreement. The Commonwealth also rallied to the common cause, supplying almost 10 per cent of the pilots in the Battle of Britain, fighting in North Africa, Italy and Asia. Many Australians fell into Japanese captivity and the Fall of Singapore left Australia vulnerable. The US began to pick up the Imperial mantle despite Franklin D. Roosevelt's aversion to all things colonial.

It was this US suspicion of Churchill's love of Empire and FDR's trust of the Soviets that most sorely tested the Atlantic Alliance. Churchill went to great lengths to win and woo the American leadership and people. That he mainly succeeded was due more to the common language and shared values than to his half American parentage. He did gain their firm backing for giving priority to beating Berlin, not Tokyo, and that was what mattered most.

The values and objectives they shared were set out in the Atlantic Charter, agreed by Churchill and FDR at their naval meeting in Placentia Bay, Newfoundland on August 9th 1941, four months before the Japanese attack on Pearl Harbour brought the US into the war. The two key paragraphs of a document that rightly has its place as a marking point on the voyage of English and the English-speaking peoples read: "They (the President of the USA and the Prime Minister) respect the right of all peoples to choose the form of government under which they will live … After the final destruction of the Nazi tyranny they hope to see established a peace … which will afford assurance that all men in all lands may live out their lives in freedom from fear and want."

This aspiration was immediately challenged by the Soviets after the "destruction of the Nazi Tyranny." The Yalta and Potsdam conferences eased the Soviet hegemony over Eastern and Central Europe but the best argument the Russians had were their armies on the ground. They had reached Berlin. Fortunately, as we have seen, the Anglo-American armies were also on the continent and in the subsequent Berlin Airlift the West's will held.

A common language and shared values were again vital. Churchill used both to alert American opinion to what was happening. At Fulton, Missouri, with President Truman sharing the platform, he coined the phrase that described so vividly the frontier of the Cold War: "From Stettin in the Baltic to Trieste in the Adriatic an iron curtain has descended across the Continent." The response he advocated was the same that he had urged in the two World Wars. The democracies, especially Britain and America, had to stand together because: "If they become divided or falter in their duty and if these all important years are allowed to slip away, then indeed catastrophe may overwhelm us all."

Truman and George Marshall did not allow the years to slip away. The Marshall Plan, which itself prefigured the initiatives taken by the Europeans themselves a few years later with the Schuman Plan, kick-started the economic and political recovery of Europe. Stalin "fell into the trap the Marshall Plan laid for him, which was to get him to build the wall that would divide Europe." The USSR found itself throughout the Cold War outspent and frequently outmaneuvered.

It is very hard to imagine what the consequences might have been of losing the Cold War. The Marshall Plan and the Berlin Airlift placed the Soviets at a major disadvantage from the start. Mao's victory in China seemed like a vast accretion of Communist power, but the USSR and China were never fully aligned. Potentially, the rift was always there and was later brilliantly exploited by Nixon and Kissinger. Had Stalin been able to take Berlin, had the Communist parties of Italy and France come to power, had Soviet missiles been permanently deployed in Cuba, had the fall of Saigon really triggered the feared "domino effect" throughout Asia – had all these catastrophes and more ever happened the West would have lost. Yet while defeat in World War II would have ended the voyage of English and extinguished freedom, Communist success in the Cold War could not have done the same.

What would have followed, however, would have been the postponement of globalization and the curtailment of the rise of English. Globalization and the rise of English are interdependent phenomena. That development began symbolically and, to a remarkable extent, practically with that voyage of three

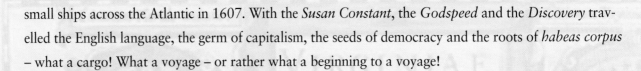

small ships across the Atlantic in 1607. With the *Susan Constant*, the *Godspeed* and the *Discovery* travelled the English language, the germ of capitalism, the seeds of democracy and the roots of *habeas corpus* – what a cargo! What a voyage – or rather what a beginning to a voyage!

The Queen's Diamond Jubilee is indeed an appropriate moment to pause on this voyage. The Queen has used the English Language throughout her reign to great effect. Monarchy invests language with moment, with significance. The film "The King's Speech" vividly portrays the challenge her father faced in mastering the spoken word and his achievement in being able to voice with such dignity the reasons for Great Britain's declaration of war on Germany in September 1939. Radio took his words into every home in Britain and to every corner of the Empire.

Throughout her reign the Queen has used the English Language to link peoples, to reinforce values and to cement friendships. She is committed to the Commonwealth and her words and manner have aided decisively the transition from Empire to Commonwealth. She has spoken of English as "The Golden Thread" binding together the diverse ethnicities and interests of a family of sovereign states. This has been because of her consistent support for and tactful insistence on the values of freedom, justice, law and enterprise. She speaks with sincerity.

It is significant and heartening that the Duke and Duchess of Cambridge have demonstrated the same quality and ability during their tour in 2011 of Canada and California.

No-where has the English Language played a more important role internationally than in fostering the friendship between the USA and Great Britain. That The Queen enjoys visiting the United States is clear. A number of both her private and State Visits testify to that. Her speeches during these State Visits and recorded in this book demonstrate very clearly how again and again she has used her words to express the values we share.

It is the good fortune of both countries that these values crucially shape the modern world, in part because they are expressed in the language that has become – to a unique extent the shared means of understanding around the Globe.

The motto of the English Speaking Union, an international educational charity, of which The Queen is Patron is "Global Understanding through English." During the past twenty years ESU activities have spread to over fifty countries, many not using English as a native tongue but all using it as a means of communications with the larger world.

Mutual understanding is the basis of citizenship to survive and evolve safe and successful societies depend on their citizen's understanding of law, enterprise and freedom. Now such understanding is vital between nations as well as within them.

It is perhaps significant that Winston Churchill, one of the great champions of the English language, was The Third Chairman of the English-Speaking Union. Of course he was also The Queen's first Prime Minister.

In the depths of the Second World War he spoke at Harvard University where he had received an Honorary Doctorate. He said that English might "become the Foundation of a common citizenship". He meant between the United States and other English speaking peoples.

It was in his view their shared "priceless inheritance." So it has proved to be. But Churchill went on to foresee a crucial contribution the English Language could make in future years "as an advantage to many races and an aid to building our new structure for preserving peace."

As we celebrate this Diamond Jubilee we should be united in our desire that this too comes to pass.

What was rumored to be the only unscripted moment of two-day visit, the Queen and Prince Philip come down the gangplank after an impromptu inspection of the reproduction Susan Constant the largest of the three ships to make the initial trip in 1606-07. Photo courtesy of the College of William and Mary Special Collections.

CHAPTER FOUR

QUEEN ELIZABETH II AT JAMESTOWN - 1957

The Jamestown Festival in 1957, which took place between April and November of that year, featured military reviews and fly-overs, ship and aircraft christenings, community-based heritage programs, an outdoor drama at Cape Henry, and a visit by Vice President Richard M. Nixon. But the 1957 commemoration is best remembered for the visit to Jamestown by the youthful Her Majesty Queen Elizabeth II, who marked the settlement's 350th anniversary with her first state visit to the United States.

Events of the festival reached their culmination in October with the visit of the British royal party on the 16th and the celebration of the Yorktown victory on the 18th and 19th. When President Eisenhower issued his invitation, her visit to the United States on the occasion of the 350th anniversary could therefore be timed to follow the Canadian visit in mid-October.

The Queen, Prince Philip, and the official party departed from Ottawa by Royal Canadian Air Force Plane on the morning of the 16th and arrived at Patrick Henry airport at 1:30 PM.

October 16, 1957 - Queen Elizabeth and Prince Philip take their first steps on American soil, greeted by US chief of protocol Wiley Buchanan at Patrick Henry Airport in Newport News, Virginia. Courtesy of Library of Virginia.

The Queen and Virginia Governor Thomas Stanley review one of the military units assembled for her arrival at the airport. Photo courtesy of William and Mary.

British Ambassador to the US Sir Harold Caccia introduces the Queen to various American dignitaries. Photo courtesy of Library of Virginia.

Old sycamore tree, Jamestown, Va., separating the tombs of the Rev. James Blair and his wife. Sam Robinson, the guide, in attendance.

For thirty years, Sam Robinson (1901–1965) acted as sexton and guide at the Jamestown Memorial Church. No trip to Jamestown was complete without the experience of an encounter with him. Weather permitting he would sit from morning to late afternoon on a tree shaded bench in the churchyard to await visitors who happened upon him as they wandered about the town site. When a sufficient number had gathered round him, he introduced them to the site.

Courtly bearing and a knack for storytelling made Robinson a natural raconteur. He spoke in the lilting cadences and idioms of a Canadian of West Indian origin. Part legend, part invention, and part fact, his stories provided a word tour of the church and its graves. Usually, he began by describing notable features of the church and its tower. The tower, said he, was the sole building from Jamestown in its heyday. He urged his listeners to inspect its bricks that bore graffiti scratched in them by eighteenth- and nineteenth-century visitors. They should be on the lookout for the one inscribed "WHH," which were the initials of a future president of the United States. Next he drew notice to the graves and wove tales about the occupants.

The highpoint of the tour happened when he came to two tombs that were entwined in the trunk of an ancient sycamore, which he called "the mother-in-law tree." One contained the bones of the Rev'd Doctor James Blair, the founder of the College of William and Mary and long time rector of Bruton Parish Church. The other held the remains of his first wife Sarah Harrison Blair.

Robinson explained their separation this way. Sarah wed James over the strong objections of her parents, who never fully reconciled themselves to the marriage. Consequently, when she died, the family objected to her being put in their plot, and she was interred at a distance from her relations. When his time came, the Rev'd Dr. Blair asked to be buried beside Sarah, and so he was. In the years that followed his death, the sycamore sprang up between the two tombs, and as it grew, it caught up Sarah's and gradually pushed it into the Harrison family plot. Thus, Robinson concluded, although his mother-in-law could not separate Blair from her daughter while she lived, her spirit sowed the sycamore seed, and nature achieved what she could not.

That Sam Robinson filled his stories with more than a little fancy was unimportant. The thing that mattered most was his capacity to enliven history in ways that mere gazing upon old gravestones and reading plaques on church walls never could. And upon a boy who whiled away many a happy hour in his company, Robinson left two enduring marks. He was the first black man of the boy's acquaintance who made his way not by the sweat of his brow but by the labor of his intellect. And he kindled in the boy a passion for doing history as his life's calling. I was that boy.

Warren M. Billings

The Queen Visits Jamestown Park

Having traveled approximately 1 mile by motorcade from Jamestown Island, the Queen, escorted by Governor Stanley, arrives at the newly constructed Jamestown Festival Park, developed by the Commonwealth of Virginia specifically for the 350th anniversary. They walk through an honor guard of living history interpreters portraying early Virginia militia.

The Queen strolls through reproduction buildings in the recreated fort – a living history museum which continues to help facilitate an understanding of the daily experience in early Jamestown through various exhibits and interpreters. The Queen and Prince Philip observe soldiers in the recreated fort, artisans in reproduction buildings, and Indians who displayed activities associated with everyday life in their villages. Courtesy of William and Mary.

The Queen views an original copy of the Magna Carta, which, in 1215, was the first document to declare limits on a sovereign's powers. One of the four surviving copies of the great charter, the copy was loaned to the Commonwealth for this occasion. Photo courtesy of William and Mary.

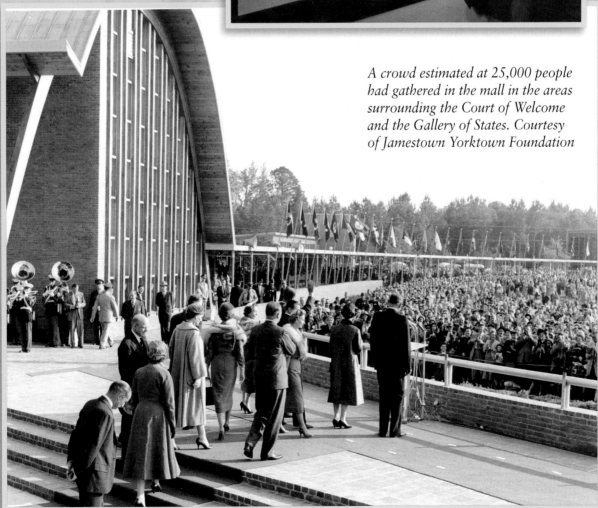

A crowd estimated at 25,000 people had gathered in the mall in the areas surrounding the Court of Welcome and the Gallery of States. Courtesy of Jamestown Yorktown Foundation

Queen Elizabeth and Prince Philip greet the crowd from the balcony on the east side of the Wren Building (circa 1695-1700) the oldest college building in the United States. The College Coat of arms, granted by the royal college of arms in May of 1694, appears on the banner hanging in front of the Queen. Courtesy of William and Mary.

Having just arrived at the College of William and Mary in Williamsburg, the Queen signs the guest register at the President's House. The house, built in 1732, is the oldest official residence for a college president in the United States. Courtesy of William and Mary.

The Queen and Prince Philip leave the President's House accompanied by the Rector of the College, James Robertson. Courtesy of William and Mary.

The Queen and Rector Robertson walk across the College Yard. Courtesy of William and Mary.

Accompanied by Mr. and Mrs. Winthrop Rockefeller, President of the Colonial Williamsburg Foundation and several coachmen, the Queen and Prince Philip leave College Corner for a ride up Duke of Gloucester Street, the restored heart of the colonial capital. Thousands of people lined the street to catch a glimpse of the royal couple as they traveled to the recreated Governor's Palace for a reception attended by 1,400 guests. Courtesy of William and Mary.

Queen Elizabeth II poses on a stairway in the Williamsburg Inn just before attending dinner in her honor on Oct. 16, 1957. Her gown is of white satin with bodice banded with embroideries of crystal, diamonds and pearls and motifs of china blue flowers mixed with moonstones and star sapphires. AP Photo

On Thursday morning, October 17th, Her Majesty and Prince Philip, accompanied by the official party, departed from Patrick Henry Airport. At 9:15 am, the President's plane took off for Washington with the royal couple aboard. Courtesy of William and Mary.

DR. WARREN M. BILLINGS

Warren M. Billings, Distinguished Professor of History, Emeritus, at the University of New Orleans is a student of colonial Virginia and Louisiana law. Widely published, his most recent books include A Law Unto Itself?: Essays in the New Louisiana Legal History (Baton Rouge, 2001), A Little Parliament The Virginia General Assembly in the Seventeenth Century (Richmond, 2004), Sir William Berkeley and the Forging of Colonial Virginia (Baton Rouge, 2004) The Papers of Sir William Berkeley, 1605–1677 (Richmond, 2007), The Old Dominion in the Seventeenth Century: A Documentary History of Virginia, 1600–1700, rev. ed. (Chapel Hill, 2007), and Magistrates and Pioneers: Essays in the History of American Law (Clark, New Jersey, 2011). His shorter works have appeared in popular magazines and such scholarly serials as Louisiana History, the Michigan Law Review, the Journal of Southern History, the Virginia Magazine of History and Biography, the William and Mary Quarterly, and Law Library Journal. He chaired Preservation Virginia's Jamestown Rediscovery Advisory Board from 1994 to 2008, was a member of Preservation Virginia's Board of Trustees from 2002 to 2008, sat on the federal Jamestown 400th Commemoration Commission from 2003 to 2008, the Board of Directors of the Louisiana State Museum from 1989 to 2004, and was Historian of the Supreme Court of Louisiana, 1982–2005. In 2002, he was Visiting Williams Professor of Law at the University of Richmond. A past fellow of the American Bar Foundation and a former Virginia Historical Society Mellon Research Fellow, he holds honorary life membership in the British and Irish Association of Law Librarians and the Company of Fellows of the Louisiana Historical Association. The Louisiana Historical Association presented him its Garnie W. McGinty Lifetime Achievement Award in 2003, and the Virginia Historical Society conferred its Richard Slattern Award for Excellence in Virginia Biography upon him in 2005. Currently, he is Visiting Professor of Law at the College of William and Mary School of Law.

CHAPTER FIVE

Dr. Warren Billings

REPRESENTATIVE GOVERNMENT

Nearly four hundred years ago, a group of colonists gathered at Jamestown on a sultry July day in 1619. Summoned by Governor-General Sir George Yeardley, they met as a "generall Assemblie." Oppressive weather and sickness forced them to adjourn after a mere five days, though not before they dealt with the public matters that occasioned their meeting. Brief though it was, that assembly gave the English their first experience of representative government in Virginia.

Contrary to myth, their exposure to representative government was something neither the settlers nor the owners of Virginia long expected nor eagerly wanted. Since 1607, the Virginia Company of London had run the colony as a quasi-military outpost, which it subjected to a harsh code of martial law. That regime chafed the colonists and failed to make a profit for the investors. By the year 1618, the place verged on failure, and in an effort to stave off its collapse the Company instituted a business plan that would transfer a more traditional British society to Virginia.

The Company introduced private land ownership, it replaced martial law with elements of English common law, and it created the general assembly. Comprised of the governor-general, company-appointed councillors of state, and burgesses elected by the free males of the colony, the assembly would convene annually. It would adopt ordinances that redressed local issues or execute mandates from London, any of which the governor-general might veto or company officers might negate. Additionally, it would also act as a court of civil and criminal justice jurisdiction.

Company officials cut the general assembly to the pattern of their own corporate structure, and they envisioned it as a subordinate body that would provide effective management of routine local matters. The play of events confounded those high hopes because the entity that became the General Assembly arose as an unintended consequence of great expectations. After 1619, the General Assembly proceeded to pass from a corporate appendage to a little Parliament to its ultimate place as the oldest continuing representative legislature in the Western Hemisphere.

The General Assembly gained in popularity once leading settlers came to regard it as a means to vibrant, if circumscribed, local governance. Those among them who became burgesses and councillors looked upon it as the forum where they might learn the arts of governance and share in running Virginia. Structurally the Assembly remained a unicameral body—that is, the governor-general, the councillors, and the burgesses all sat together and worked as a single house—which seemingly satisfied company intentions for it. So it might well have continued had not the Virginia Company bankrupted.

Bankruptcy compelled the Crown to intervene. It quashed the Company's charter of incorporation in 1624. A year later, King Charles I proclaimed Virginia a royal dominion, which altered the purpose and shape of the General Assembly forevermore. Destruction of the charter destroyed the Assembly's legal basis for its being. Charles inadvertently threw it into even deeper constitutional limbo when he failed to recognize its existence in his proclamation. Moreover, Charles's subsequent inattention left the settlers to their own devices legislatively. His oversight gave them an enormous, if not always welcomed, latitude to develop the General Assembly.

After 1624, the royal governors-general continued to call the Assembly to enact needed legislation, thereby establishing a precedent for its continuation. They also joined with influential colonists who insistently pressed Charles I to legitimate the body. Such doggedness succeeded in 1639 when the king commissioned Sir Francis Wyatt governor-general and sanctioned future yearly meetings of the Assembly. By then, the Assembly was already Virginia's principal lawgiver. It resembled Parliament somewhat more than it had in 1619, but it still remained unicameral and rather formless. Internally, it controlled who sat as burgesses and defined some of its procedures. Its legislative reach touched wide areas of colonial life as members arrogated increasingly broad powers to themselves and as they themselves grew to be more mindful of its possibilities.

A significant milepost along the road to a Virginia tradition of representative government happened early in the tenure of Wyatt's successor, Sir William Berkeley. Berkeley, who suddenly displaced Sir Francis, arrived unannounced at Jamestown with few allies. When he called the General Assembly of March 1643, he meant to build a following among the burgesses so he suggested that they should become a House of Burgesses that sat apart from him and his councillors. The burgesses responded eagerly to his urging. And now the General Assembly separated into two houses, each of which gradually assumed differing responsibilities. Thus, dividing the Assembly kindled the idea of separation of powers that eventually became an integral element in the Virginia Declaration of Rights of 1776, later Virginia state constitutions, and the federal Constitution itself. It is therefore no reach of fancy to assert that the General Assembly of March 1643 was every bit as significant as the one that Sir George Yeardley convened twenty-five years before, if not more so.

After 1643, assemblymen looked increasingly to Parliament, its officers, and its procedures for guidance about making the General Assembly work as a legislative institution. They acquired more authority because Berkeley encouraged them as he threw in with the great planters who filled the Council of State and the House of Burgesses and who controlled local government as well. Discontinuities bred by the Civil War in the British Isles, the Anglo-Powhatan War of 1644–1646, and years of parliamentary rule after Berkeley's overthrow in 1652 also contributed to the Assembly's rising importance, and those tumults also imbued the members with deeper feelings of their pre-eminence too. As a result, the Assembly's transit to a little Parliament was all but complete when Berkeley again returned as governor-general in 1660. By no means inclined to arrest the trend, he actually promoted it to the point that General Assemblies of the 1660s and 1670s assumed powers that surpassed those of the Parliament in Westminster.

The Crown mostly ignored the significance of those developments because King Charles II let Berkeley run the Old Dominion pretty much as he saw fit. Bacon's Rebellion in 1676 changed that royal indifference, however. The revolt destroyed Berkeley politically and forced Charles and his minions to intervene in Virginia, as the Crown had not since the 1620s. Throughout the 1680s and the 1690s, they purposefully undercut the Assembly in ways that diminished it significantly and ushered in an era of dominance by the governor-general and the Council of State. As a result, the Assembly lost its freedom of annual sessions, its prerogative to act as a high court of appeals, its liberty to choose it clerks, and its nearly absolute right of legislation.

Royal interference did not go unchallenged. Indeed, Whitehall's reach for ascendancy provoked sharp protests, especially from the burgesses who bewailed the assaults on their "ancient" privileges. Grudgingly, they yielded to a force they could not overbear and acceded to a recalibration of their relationship with the Crown that moved the thrust the Anglo-Virginia politics from indifference to concern for broader imperial issues. The overthrow of King James II and war with France slowed the incursions, but the likelihood of future infringements remained a distinct possibility. So did the fear that an aggressive Crown and assertive governors-general would someday result in an acutely dangerous strengthening of royal power. After 1700, squabbles that erupted eventually blossomed into irreparable confrontations between the House of Burgesses and Parliament and led to independence.

Two sources of talent filled the General Assembly. The governors-general all hailed from the upper levels of British society, and they were closely tied to the Crown. Theirs was a challenging responsibility in that they had to govern in the interests of their royal masters and the colonists, and those interests diverged as often as they coincided. Governor-General Berkeley resolved the conundrum by determining that what was best for Virginia was best for the Crown too, which was why he boosted the growth of the Assembly. His successors put the interests of the Crown first and foremost, and that choice caused friction between the executive and the Assembly that endured for the remainder of the colonial era.

The councillors of state and the burgesses belonged to an elite class of colonists. Related to one another by kinship and common interests, they stood at the apex of colonial society. A chair at the council table was the highest place to which any of them might aspire, and gaining one of those seats represented the culmination of years of political experience. Burgesses on the other hand held the only elected office in Virginia.

No member of the General Assembly served a fixed term of office. Both the governors-general and councillors of state were royal appointees, meaning that they kept their places at the king's pleasure or until there was a change in reigns. Initially, burgesses represented a hodge-podge of constituencies: private plantations, church parishes, boroughs, counties, and any other precinct whose electors were willing to compensate burgesses for their services. Following its institution of the county court system of local government in the 1630s, the General Assembly began turning the counties into the basic electoral unit and the political foundation for the colony's governing classes. It finished the transformation in 1662, when it restricted representation to the counties and to Jamestown. Likewise, it levied a stiff monetary penalty on any county where the voters neglected to elect the required two burgesses. Later on, the Assembly allowed voters in Williamsburg, Norfolk, and the College of William and Mary each to elect a burgess of their own. After the capital removed to Williamsburg, Jamestown remained a constituency, which rendered it the nearest thing to a rotten borough in Virginia before 1776.

What is noteworthy about these arrangements is this. Equating representation with voters who lived in specific geographic political subdivision was a colonial Virginia practice that inspired the modern American notion of a representation. Nowadays whether that person is an elected local official, a state legislator, or member of Congress, his or her duty, first and foremost, is to the voters of the district that put him or her in office. In the seventeenth century, however, the view prevailed in England that a member of the House of Commons spoke for the entire body politic and not exclusively for the particular electors who sent him to Parliament. No one took notice of the difference until it became an issue in the constitutional crises that led to the Revolution.

The governor-general controlled the timing of elections to the House of Burgesses. He directed a writ that ordered county sheriffs to conduct the poll and to certify the results. There were no campaigns, nor were elections contested until the eighteenth century. Voters cast their preferences orally. A voter could vote in as many counties as he qualified as an elector, which is why polling lasted several days.

Qualifications for voting and standing for the House of Burgesses originated in the colony's earliest days. Burgesses were invariably substantial landowners, although during much of the seventeenth century any free adult male could vote irrespective of whether he owned land. The first restriction on the franchise came in 1670, when the General Assembly limited it to landholders and ratepayers on theory that "the lawes of England grant a voyce . . . only to such as by their estates real or personall have interest enough to tye them to the endeavour of the publique good." Governor-General Berkeley suspended the statute in the election of 1676 only to have it reinstated by the express command of King Charles II. Later laws stiffened the requirements still further by, for example, denying a vote to Roman Catholics or to free African Virginians and by increasing the amount of property needed to become a voter. Indeed, the visible stake in society principal continued until the Virginia constitution of 1851 finally abolished it.

Franchise laws, like all other acts of the General Assembly, spoke to their makers' outlook on the nature of things. Stuart Britons as a general rule believed in a polity grounded in authority, order, rank, and submission to one's betters as God-given, and for them monarchy was its bedrock. They took for granted that an exalted few were divinely ordained to dictate the fate of the underprivileged many. A free press was nonexistent. There was no toleration of dissent, religious or political. Free speech was no liberty, and private thought could be deemed as treachery too. Women were regarded as inferior beings and therefore unfit to govern. Men without a visible stake in society; that is, real property, were disenfranchised. Having a vote was no license to run for the House of Commons, however, because seats there belonged to men who were of England's ruling classes. Those individuals commanded and received the obedience of inferior sorts, and none of them solicited the "public" opinion because the views of the ordinary subject counted for nothing. Across the seventeenth century, Englishmen on both sides of the Atlantic inquired deeply into these ageless assumptions as monarch and subject disputed one another over whether the ultimate power to rule the realm lay with the sovereign or with Parliament.

Assemblymen drew inspiration from that rich heritage, taking from it what they remembered and blended those remembrances with their Virginia experiences. Virginia was a place of fresh starts where the lucky few, like themselves, could pursue dreams of aggrandizement unfettered by the constraints of the Old World. Freedom had its limits. If they were to render Virginia civil, then they must bind their society by rules of their making. The hunt for appropriate statutory means of resolving legal disagreements, raising taxes, and protecting one another provided its own abundant impulses to explore the intricacies of power and modes of governance. Consequently, it was this mix of memory, necessity, deliberate borrowing, and frequent experimentation that slowly gave shape and figure to the General Assembly.

The General Assembly had come a great distance since its first meeting, which made representative government a well-established feature of life in colonial Virginia when the 1600s drew to a close. No one on the British side of the Atlantic questioned its existence, despite the Crown's recent hedging it in. It still looked like Parliament in many respects, and the resemblance would come nearer during the eighteenth century as the burgesses regained some of what they lost in the 1680s and 1690s. In a real sense, their quest for power duplicated the journey of the House of Commons in its struggles with the Stuart monarchs, and both arrived at similar destinations. What remained very much in doubt, however, was the constitutional matter of how the General Assembly and Virginia law related to Parliament and English law. Neither the English nor the Virginians paid scant heed to the issue much before the 1760s, by which time Parliament asserted it right to legislate for the empire in all cases whatsoever. That claim of absolute legislative supremacy threatened the very existence of the General Assembly. Parliament would not give way, the Virginians revolted, and independence ushered in the next phase of representative government in the Old Dominion.

CHAPTER SIX

QUEEN ELIZABETH AT CHARLOTTESVILLE - 1976

As part of the 1976 celebration to commemorate American independence, Queen Elizabeth II was invited to tour appropriate sites along the east coast associated with the American Revolution. She accepted the invitation of the Virginia Independence Commission and visited Charlottesville just 6 days after the July 4th penultimate date.

At 11:35 on the morning of Saturday, July 10th, 1976, she and H.R.H. Prince Philip landed at Charlottesville Airport and were greeted by Governor and Mrs. Mills Godwin and British Counsel General Geoffrey L. and Mrs. Scullard. They traveled via motorcade together into Charlottesville, arriving at the University of Virginia to be greeted by University President and Mrs. Frank Herford. On a platform built for the occasion on the front of Cabell Hall, the Queen addressed the gathered crowd with brief remarks and presented the Commonwealth of Virginia with a devisal (coat of arms) of the arms used by the Virginia Company of London and later by the Royal Colony and Dominion of Virginia. Governor Godwin presented the Queen with a specially bound copy of Dumas Malone's "Jefferson" which won the 1975 Pulitzer Prize. Dr. Malone was a member of the University's faculty. Immediately afterwards, she and Prince Phillip crisscrossed the Lawn, making their way towards the Rotunda with University President and Mrs. Frank Hereford and paid a brief visit to a student room on the Lawn as well as Pavilion I. Coming out of Pavilion I, the official party went to the Rotunda where they were greeted by a number of dignitaries and then went up the stairs to the Dome Room for a luncheon hosted by the Governor and attended by 134 guests. After lunch, the Queen and Governor Godwin stood at the top of the stairs of the newly restored building, turned to the crowd to wave, and then left the Jefferson-designed "Academical Village."

Her Majesty and the Governor motorcaded through the streets of Charlottesville to the Western Virginia Bicentennial Center near Monticello. In a brief stop they saw several exhibits, and she and the Prince planted trees outside of the Center.

The party went up to Monticello where The Queen was presented to members of the Board of Trustees of the Thomas Jefferson Memorial Foundation. She was then given a private tour by James Bear, Curator for the Foundation, and Historian Fredrick Nichols. When the interior tour was completed, she walked to the outbuilding known as Col. Randolph's Office. She stepped onto the lawn of Jefferson's home and was greeted by members of the Virginia General Assembly. At the end of the stroll, she was presented with a gift. She returned to the Charlottesville Airport and departed at 3:00 that afternoon.

Queen Elizabeth II strolls along the Lawn at the University of Virginia. Photo by Jayne Hushen.

In the front of Cabell Hall, the Queen gave brief remarks and presented the Commonwealth of Virginia with a devisal of the coat of arms used by the Virginia Company of London and later by the Royal Colony and Dominion of Virginia. Seated behind Her Majesty is Frank Hereford, President of the University of Virginia.

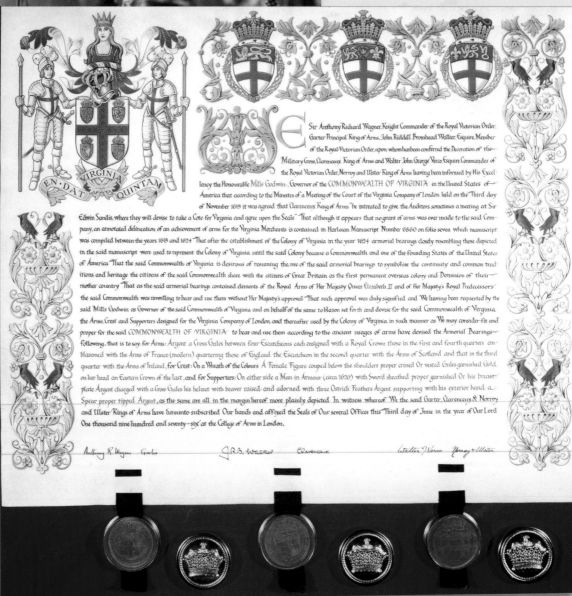

The Queen and Governor Godwin strolled up towards the Rotunda and paid a brief visit to student rooms on the Lawn as well as Pavilion 1.

Inside the first floor of the Rotunda, the Queen greeted University Law Professor and constitutional expert A. E. 'Dick' Howard

Upstairs in the Dome Room – the room Jefferson designed to be used as the University's library, a luncheon was held, hosted by the Governor and attended by approximately 130 guests.

While touring Thomas Jefferson's Monticello home Queen Elizabeth II as pictured in the former President's bedroom with the canopied bed in the foreground on July 10, 1976 in Charlottesville. With the Queen on the left is historian Frederick Nichols and at right is James Bear, curator of the Jefferson Museum. AP Photo

At the Western Virginia Bicentennial Center, Queen Elizabeth turns the soil to plant a tree to commemorate her visit.

After the tour of the interior of Monticello, the Queen stepped onto the lawn of Jefferson's home and was greeted by members of the Virginia General Assembly, the oldest legislative body in the Western hemisphere.

In the sixty years since becoming Queen in 1952, Queen Elizabeth II has visited the United States on many occasions. Beginning with her first visit as Queen in 1957, her presence on American soil sparks excitement and celebration.

In October 1957, she made her first official state visit to Washington, D.C. and attended the 350th anniversary of the settlement of Jamestown with a visit to Williamsburg. Before sailing back to the United Kingdom, she visited New York City.

In July 1976, she returned for a state visit to Washington and toured the United States east coast in conjunction with the United States Bicentennial celebrations aboard HMY Britannia. Stops included Philadelphia, Washington D.C., New York City, Charlottesville (Virginia), Newport and Providence (Rhode Island), and Boston. While in Philadelphia, she rang the Liberty Bell, in Charlottesville, she visited Thomas Jefferson's Monticello and in Boston she attended a special service at Old North Church.

In late February to early March 1983, Queen Elizabeth toured the United States west coast aboard HMY Britannia, and made a private visit to Ronald Reagan's retreat in the Santa Ynez Mountains, Rancho del Cielo. Stops included San Diego, Palm Springs, Los Angeles, Santa Barbara, San Francisco, Yosemite National Park (California), and Seattle (Washington).

THE QUEEN IN BOSTON

Queen Elizabeth II and Prince Philip attend a special service at Old North Church in Boston, Mass., Sunday, July 11, 1976. It is the first visit of a reigning British monarch to Massachusetts.
AP Photo

THE QUEEN IN FLORIDA

Queen Elizabeth II awards General Norman Schwarzkopf the title of honorary Knight Commander in the Military Division of the most honorable Order of the Bath in Tampa, Florida. The award is the highest honor Britain can bestow on a foreigner.
1991 AP Photo/Scott Iskowitz

In 1984 and 1986, she traveled to Kentucky searching for a thoroughbred prospect to win the English Derby and visited Ambassador and Mrs. Will Farish at their farm.

In May 1991, Her Majesty returned for a state visit to Washington D.C. and addressed a joint session of the United States Congress. She made a private visit to Kentucky, and also toured the southern United States with stops including Baltimore (Maryland), Miami and Tampa (Florida), Austin, San Antonio, and Houston (Texas).

In May 2007, she paid a state visit to Washington D.C., addressed the Virginia General Assembly, attended the official ceremonies of the 400th anniversary of the establishment of Jamestown, toured NASA's Goddard Space Flight Center, visited the National World War II Memorial on the National Mall, and made a private visit to Kentucky to attend the Kentucky Derby for the first time.

On July 6, 2010, Queen Elizabeth returned to New York City, visited the United Nations and laid a wreath at Ground Zero.

THE QUEEN IN CHICAGO

Pomp and circumstance and a flourish by a Marine Corps band greet Queen Elizabeth II on July 6, 1959 at the entrance to Chicago's International Trade Fair. AP Photo/J. Walter Green

THE QUEEN IN LOS ANGELES

Queen Elizabeth II shakes hands with singer Frank Sinatra (Perry Como and Dionne Warwick are also pictured) in Los Angeles in 1983.
Photo by Anwar Hussein/Getty Images

THE QUEEN IN MARYLAND

Queen Elizabeth II and NASA astronaut Mike Foale talk to astronauts aboard the International Space Station, during a tour of the NASA Goddard Space Center in Greenbelt, Maryland in 2007.
AP Photo/Timothy Clary, pool

THE QUEEN AT GROUND ZERO

Queen Elizabeth II places a wreath in remembrance of the victims of the Sept. 11, 2001 terrorist attacks on the World Trade Center site, Tuesday, July 6, 2010 in New York.
AP Photo/Fred R. Conrad, Pool

THE QUEEN IN KENTUCKY

Queen Elizabeth II, center, looks at stallions at Lane's End Farm in Kentucky in May 1991. The Queen is accompanied by Lord Porchester, rear, Sarah Farish, right, and Will Farish, left, behind the horse. AP Photo/Lexington Herald-Leader, David Perry

THE QUEEN IN SAN FRANCISCO

A sailor exchanges smiles with Queen Elizabeth II and Prince Philip on their return to the HMY Britannia on March 5, 1983 in San Francisco. AP Photo

THE QUEEN IN YOSEMITE

Park superintendent Bob Binnewies points out highlights from Inspiration Point to Queen Elizabeth II during her visit to Yosemite National Park in California in 1983. AP Photo/Walt Zeboski

THE RT. HON. LORD HOWELL OF GUILDFORD, PC

David Howell - The Right Honorable Lord Howell of Guildford - is a former Secretary of State for Energy and for Transport in the UK Government and an economist and journalist.

Currently he is the House of Lords Deputy Leader of the Opposition, and Foreign Affairs Spokesman. David Howell has been President of the British Institute of Energy Economists since 2003. He is also a Member of the Financial Advisory Board to The Kuwait Investment Authority as well as the European Consultant to Japan Central Railway Co. and to Mitsubishi Electric, Europe BV.

David Howell is a regular columnist in the Japan Times and an occasional columnist in the Wall Street Journal and the International Herald Tribune. He is the author of twelve political pamphlets and four books, Blind Victory, Freedom and Capital, The Edge of Now and Out of the Energy Labyrinth.

David Howell was educated at Eton and King's College Cambridge. He has been Trustee of Shakespeare's Globe Theatre since 2000.

CHAPTER EIGHT

Judge J. Harvie Wilkinson III

RULE OF LAW

The rule of law has been so much a feature of Anglo-American life that we take it for granted. But the idea that kings and presidents should be subjects of the law is the most radical – and the most hopeful – idea of modern times. Without it, power is left to work its will, and freedom is destined to perish.

It is true, to be sure, that law helps to ensure order. Law functions as the great alternative to bloodshed. If a people can find justice in the courts, they will be less likely to seek redress in the streets.

With order comes freedom. Freedom from fear. Freedom to move about. But law confers so many other benefits of order. It orders the holding of property, the making of contracts, the formation and dissolution of family relationships, the collection and disbursement of public revenues and so much more. It is the order imparted by law to society that has long helped the people of the United States and Britain fulfill their potential and achieve a decent prosperity.

But law aspires to more than order. It seeks an even higher form of liberty. Whether embedded in constitutions or in centuries of custom, law confers inalienable rights against the state. Among those are the freedoms of speech and religious exercise, the right to be free from unreasonable searches and seizures, and the great trial rights – to counsel, to a jury of one's peers, to call supportive witnesses, and to confront adverse ones.

Each of these rights boasts its own virtues. Free speech educates citizens, protects unpopular ideas, and makes sure democracy hears everybody out. Freedom of religion means government plays no favorites in matters of faith. As the First Amendment to the American Constitution safeguards matters of expression and conscience, so the Fourth Amendment protects hearth, home, and personal conversation from the baseless intrusions of the state. The Sixth Amendment guarantees that detention of the citizen is not a matter of executive fancy but of the government's sober burden of proof. The accused has not only counsel as his champion, but also the right of cross-examination, which the Supreme Court has recognized as the "greatest legal engine ever invented for the discovery of truth."

Liberty must reside in more than written parchment. As Judge Learned Hand wrote, liberty lives "in the hearts of men and women." If it dies there, "no constitution, no law, no court can save it." Liberty is the keepsake of the people even more than the sacred trust of courts. It has flourished in Britain and America because each generation was willing to nourish it, to protest its abridgement, and to hand it down through the centuries as devotedly as property is passed through written will. The American Revolution was fought in part for the liberty and lawful rights of Englishmen – even as we sought independence, we acknowledged those imperishable freedoms Great Britain had done so much to bring about.

It is worth thinking what a world without constitutional liberty would be like. One need only remember the fates that the monstrous tyrants of the twentieth century visited upon their people in order to appreciate the rule of law. For those totalitarian states were worlds without restraint, worlds where the law, the courts, the press, and the honest processes of democracy had ceased to function, worlds where dread and suspicion marked even the most routine interactions among citizens.

America and Britain were able to resist the scourge of fascism and communism not just by drawing upon their material resources, not just by displaying uncommon valor and courage, but through their knowledge of the contrast between a world of liberty under law and the kind of world that Hitler, Stalin and their like were seeking to bring about. In that sense, the rule of law became for our two countries a flag of battle, something to live by and to die for, something that along with family, friends and countrymen gave meaning to the sacrifice that thousands upon thousands of soldiers and civilians made willingly day-in and day-out.

So we honor our ancestors and keep faith with our descendants by renewing in our time our forebears' timeless gift. To understand the rule of law, one must appreciate not just its possibilities, but its limits and constraints. Constitutional law by and large does not confer economic entitlements. It lays down a framework of government, not a prescription for policy. Budgetary matters and foreign policy decisions, for example, are for the people's representatives. That is as it should be. The rule of law must never be disdainful of popular sovereignty. Judicial authority is meant to support self-governance, not to supplant it. Just as popular majorities can infringe minority rights, so too can judges usurp majority prerogatives. Either course inflicts inestimable damage upon the rule of law.

The rule of law is not only meant to be supportive of democracy. It buttresses a capitalist economy as well. Commercial enterprise requires legal stability and predictability. Without legal stability, companies and individuals cannot properly assess the elements of economic risk. Independent courts help to provide this stability – they interpret contracts, work to ensure market integrity, and protect all forms of property according to rules and not whim or caprice. It is not too much to say that the great Anglo-America traditions of democratic liberty and economic freedom would not have flourished without a stable legal order and independent courts.

The independence of courts should never be taken for granted. In many countries, the court system is corrupt and judges are subject to intimidation from the powerful and the fanatical alike. Citizens know when this is so. In talking with visiting delegations from many different countries, I sense their yearning for an environment where judges will act fearlessly and free of racial, religious, or partisan prejudice. The life tenure and protection against salary reductions afforded federal judges in America may not be the only way to ensure judicial independence, but some mechanism must be in place. Many elected state judges display great integrity and courage in their rulings, but the vulnerability of court systems to large inflows of campaign cash is a growing problem that must not be overlooked.

The rule of law must be more than a rhetorical exercise. In a sense, it lives or dies in practice. The public workers we too pejoratively dismiss as bureaucrats will decide the fate of law along with courts. Do citizen interactions with their government bear the earmarks of efficiency, courtesy, human dignity and respect? The postal worker, the police officer, the clerk at the Department of Motor Vehicles, the IRS employee, are all tribunes of the law and carry out its edicts. Do our dealings with them leave us with a sense of appreciation and gratitude or with a sour taste? In hundreds upon thousands of daily transactions, the law proves itself or it does not. It is inseparable from the men and women to whose care and judgment we entrust it.

Law is founded finally upon the ideal of citizenship. Law exists in part because each of us is far from perfect. Still, the question persists: Do we seek to cheat on law or to observe it? Do we obey speed limits? Do we pay the taxes that are due and owing? But law is not just obedience but participation. Do we serve on juries? Do we petition and debate? Do we vote? If so, we give to law its life. The rule of law is not a gift one passively receives, but something each citizen must actively return. It is a compact between citizen and state. Great Britain and America have always regarded it as such. Our two countries understand this above all – at the end of the day, the rule of law is us.

Four members of Native Virginia Tribes dance in front of Cobham Hall, a country house in Kent, England. A manor house has been on the site since the 12th century.

CHAPTER NINE

2006
VIRGINIA DELEGATIONS TRAVEL TO ENGLAND

With royal charter in hand and financing finally in place, the London Company's leaders hastened to assemble the ships, crew and settlers for the historic expedition. So it was, on December 19, 1606, on the approach of the winter solstice and with little fanfare, that the expedition left Blackwall Pier and set sail for Virginia. Of the passengers, 105 were settlers, the rest crew. About half the passengers were gentlemen from the upper end of English society. But there also were tradesmen and professionals, including four carpenters, 12 laborers, a blacksmith, a mason, a bricklayer, a tailor, a barber, a drummer and a chirugeon (precursor of a medical technician).

On December 19th 2006, re-enactors depict gentlemen of the early 1600's and greet visitors to the Dockland's Museum in London for the 400th anniversary of the departure of the three ships.

The largest of the ships, at 100 tons and with 71 passengers and crew, was the Susan Constant, captained by Christopher Newport, the fleet's overall commander. The Godspeed (40 tons, with 52 passengers and crew), was led by Capt. Bartholomew Gosnold, the vice-admiral of the fleet. The Discovery, a 20-ton pinnace, carried 21 passengers and crew under the command of John Ratcliffe.

A variety of observances were held in London on December 19, 2006 to mark the anniversary of the ships' departure for Jamestown. The reproduction Discovery was taken to Canary Wharf, London, adjacent to the Museum in Docklands, where a new exhibit about Jamestown ("Journey to the New World") opened.

The Discovery remained there until the exhibition's close in May 2007,

Rebecca Casson, Executive Director of the British Jamestown Committee, stands at the bow of the reproduction ship Discovery. Discovery was the smallest of the three ships to cross the Atlantic in 1607, leaving from a site very near where this picture was taken in London.

and then it commenced a four-month tour that took it to festivals and other events at Dover, Chatham, Lincoln, Bristol, Ipswich (Suffolk) and Harwich (Essex). More than 340,000 visitors came to see it, and an estimated 6.9 million saw media coverage of its visit.

An honor guard with members from both Colonial Williamsburg and Virginia Military Institute solemnly escort dignitaries from the Docklands Museum to the adjacent wharf to lay wreaths on the reproduction of the ship Discovery.

Among those attending events at Canary Wharf – a mile from the site of the departure of the three ships - were three Americans— Virginia Governor Tim Kaine, Stephen Adkins, Chief of Virginia's Chickahominy Indians , and American Ambassador to the UK Robert Tuttle—who visited the Docklands museum with other dignitaries as part of the ceremonies on December 19, 2006, marking the 400th anniversary of the three ships' departure for Jamestown.

The American delegation in a private wreath-laying ceremony at Virginia Quay, near Blackwall, where a monument marks the place from which the 104 settlers departed in December 1606 bound for Virginia.

Governor Tim Kaine, Chief Stephen Adkins and Ambassador Robert Tuttle chat before ceremonies on December 19 2006.

Media interest was high on both sides of the Atlantic for events in London in December 2006. Here Virginia Governor Tim Kaine talks to British and American correspondents based in London.

Virginians attending the December 19, 2006 events marking the 400th anniversary of the launch of the Susan Constant, Godspeed, and Discovery prepare to lay wreaths at the Virginia Quay monument honoring the original voyagers

The exact site of the departure of the three ships from Blackwall is marked by a monument that was unveiled in 1928 by America's Ambassador. Here the monument is covered with flowers 400 years to the day after the departure of the voyage.

Guests at the packed Great Hall of Middle Temple on December 19, 2006, listen as Governor Kaine delivers remarks on the historic significance of the Jamestown voyage and settlement.

National colors were presented by honor guards consisting of cadets from the Virginia Military Institute and the London Unified Officer Training Corps.

After Governor Kaine deliverd memorable remarks at Middle Temple he talks to Lord Phillips. Lord Phillips traveled to Virginia for several commorative events.

The day concluded with a formal dinner that evening at the Middle Temple – the site where the Virginia Company's charter was issued - hosted by the Federal Jamestown 2007 Commemoration Commission. Interest in the occasion soared after the Queen's announcement that she would visit the United States in 2007. The hundreds who were able to attend the sell-out event heard a stirring keynote address from Lord Chief Justice Phillips of Worth Matravers, himself a master of the Middle Temple, as well as moving remarks by Governor Kaine, toasts by Lord Watson and Virginia Delegate Vincent F. Callahan, Jr., a preview of plans for the Royal Visit and Anniversary Weekend by Virginia House Speaker William J. Howell, and a benediction by Chief Adkins. Color guards from Virginia Military Institute and the London Unified Officer Training Corps presented the colors, after which both national anthems were played. Reverend Robin Griffith-Jones, Master of the Temple Church, delivered the invoca-

A cadet from Virginia Military Institute serves as a member of the honor guard as Governor Kaine, speaking at the Museum in Docklands on December 19, 2006, transfers ownership of the replica ship Discovery to the Jamestown UK Foundation

tion. Dinner guests received a commemorative clock as a memento, along with a copy of Lord Watson's new book, Jamestown: The Journey of English, and a keepsake program that included Commissioner Gleason's manuscript, "The Beginning of Jamestown: The Royal Charter, Blackwall and the Voyage to Virginia."

Lord Phillips of Worth Matravers, the Lord Chief Justice of England and Wales, holds a copy of Lord Watson's book, Jamestown: The Voyage of English, as he delivers keynote remarks at Middle Temple during the Federal Commission's gala dinner commemorating the 400th anniversary of the launch of the original voyage to Jamestown.

Speaker Howell describes plans for the 400th anniversary commemoration at Jamestown, including visits by Her Majesty and the American President, and invites Britons to Virginia for the festivities.

Keith Smith, a representative of the Nansemond Tribe, shows his regalia as well as dexterity at the Big Day Out Festival in Gravesend England.

On July 14, 2006, a 55-member Virginia Indian delegation that included five tribal chiefs, and representatives of all eight state-recognized tribes arrived in England for nearly a week of educational and cultural activities that drew extensive media coverage there and significant notice in the United States. It was to be the tribes' first official mission to England in more than two centuries, and it called to mind the dramatic visit of Pocahontas in 1617. The delegation was welcomed at Cobham Hall in the Borough of Gravesham by Allan Willett CMG, Lord Lieutenant of Kent, who represented Her Majesty Queen Elizabeth II. After a procession in which the visiting Indians entered the hall in native regalia bearing the flags of the United States, Virginia, and each of the eight tribes, Chief Anne Richardson of the Rappahannock Tribe spoke movingly of the Virginia Indians' journey over four centuries marked by tragedy, survival, and, more recently, renewed hopefulness. She presented the Lord Lieutenant with a gold wedding ring, a gift for the Queen that symbolized the tribes continual relationship with the Crown since the 1677 treaty and their affection for Her Majesty. Later, the tribal delegation went to the town of Gravesend for a private worship service at St. George's Church, the final resting place of Pocahontas.

Leaders and members of the Virginia Indian tribes are joined by representatives of Her Majesty, Queen Elizabeth II, the U.S. Embassy, British and Kentish governments, and British and American commemoration planning committees at Cobham Hall in Kent for the official welcoming ceremony on July 14, 2006

Pocahontas died as she, her husband John Rolfe, and their young son Thomas were en route down the Thames on their return voyage to Virginia in March 1617. She was buried in the chancel area of St. George's Church, where stained glass windows donated by the Colonial Dames of America in 1914 still honor her memory. In the churchyard stands a statue of Pocahontas that is identical to the one outside the Memorial Church at Historic Jamestowne.

Allan Willett, Lord-Lieutenant of Kent, welcomes Chief Anne Richardson of the Rappahannock Indian Tribe at Cobham Hall in Kent during the Virginia Indians' July 2006 mission to England.

They returned to the church two days later for a public worship service, where they were joined by 250 parishioners, local government leaders, and members of the Jamestown 2007 British Committee.

The Kentish Borough of Gravesham was also the scene of a two-day cultural festival in which the native visitors donned their traditional regalia, performed songs and dances, held a pow-wow, displayed arts and crafts, and mingled with the estimated 12,000 English visitors who attended the popular event. The Indians continued their educational and cultural outreach for several days thereafter, visiting 16 primary and secondary schools in the borough, participating in a cultural diversity seminar hosted by the Kent County Council, and joining early Virginia history scholars, 17th-century-expert Dr. Warren M. Billings, and Dr. Helen Roundtree, for a University of Kent symposium at Canterbury. The chiefs, other tribal representatives and several representatives from the Jamestown Commemoration concluded the successful mission on July 19 with a visit to London, where they toured Parliament, viewed Prime Minister's Question Time from the Distinguished Visitors Gallery, visited the British Museum, and attended other significant meetings and functions.

"Life has not been easy for Virginia's indigenous peoples," wrote Steve Adkins, Chief of the Chickahominy Tribe, in a commentary published the week before the Jamestown anniversary in May 2007, "but to the person we are proud to be Virginians and Americans. Most tribal members across the Commonwealth are proud to be a part of a commemoration that has provided an opportunity for us to tell our story and to let the world know that descendants of some of the sovereign nations who greeted the settlers on the shores of the Powhatan River (James River) at Tsenacomoco are still here."

Representatives of Virginia Indian tribes perform traditional dance in Native regalia for Gravesham festival-goers during the tribes' historic mission and educational outreach in England, July 2006.

Responding to the hospitality of the British hosts, native Virginian drummers play on the grounds of Cobham Hall after the welcoming ceremony.

Virginia Indians visiting England in July 2006 gather in front of the monument to Pocahontas on the grounds of St. George's Church at Gravesend, where the revered princess was buried in 1617.

The Indians continued educational outreach for several days with small groups visiting 16 primary and secondary schools in the borough, where they displayed their musical and artistic expertise to nearly 10,000 students.

Representatives of all Virginia tribes participated in a cultural diversity seminar hosted by the Kent County Council to shed light on the 4 centuries of interaction between cultures to Kent governmental leaders.

Representatives of the 8 Virginia Indian Tribes stand outside the Houses of Parliament and are greeted by the 'Father' (longest serving member) of the House of Commons, the Rt. Hon. Alan Williams. This was the final day of their week-long visit to England in July, 2006.

Meeting with the Rt. Hon. Michael Martin, Speaker of the House of Commons, in the historic Speakers Chambers in the houses of Parliament are Chief Ken Adams, Chief of the Upper Mattaponi, Warren Cook, the Chief of the Pamunkey, Chief Gene W. Adkins of the Eastern Division Chickahominy Indians, and Keith Smith, a representative of the Nansemond Tribe.

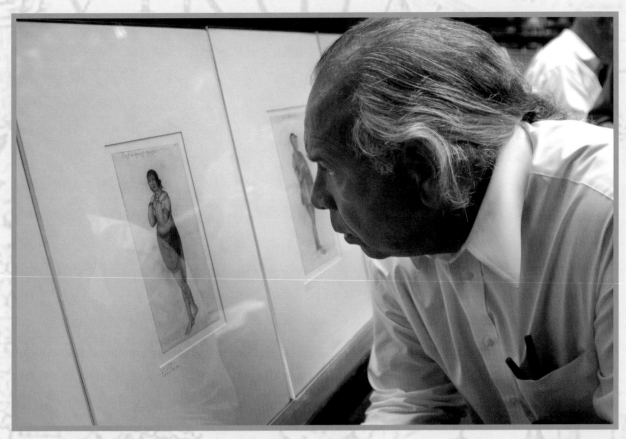

At the British museum Ken Adams Chief of the Upper Mattaponi tribe closely examines an original John White drawing of a Native American – possibly of one of his ancestors

Viscountess Penelope Cobham (third from right) hosted a reception at the Houses of Parliament for the Virginia Indian leadership that visited London.

RICHARD L. OLVER

Dick Olver was appointed Chairman of BAE Systems plc in July 2004.

Prior to that he was Deputy Group Chief Executive of BP plc from January 2003. Dick was appointed to the Board of BP and became Chief Executive, Exploration and Production in January 1998. He continued his association with BP as Deputy Chairman of TNK-BP from July 2004 until October 2006.

Dick joined BP in 1973 and held a wide variety of positions in the upstream oil and gas business as well as Corporate planning and strategy.

He is a chartered engineer with a First Class Honours degree in Civil Engineering and is also a Fellow of the Institution of Civil Engineers. In November 2004 Dick was awarded an Honorary Doctorate in Science from City University, London and in July 2005 he was elected a Fellow of the Royal Academy of Engineering and subsequently served on their Council from July 2006 to July 2009. In June 2006 he was awarded an Honorary Doctorate in Science from Cranfield University, Bedfordshire and in October 2001 he became a Fellow of the City & Guilds of London Institute

Dick is an Adviser to Clayton, Dubilier and Rice and HSBC. He is a member of both the Prime Minister's Business Advisory Group and the India/UK CEO Forum. Dick is also a member of the Multi National Chairmen's Group (MNCG). He is also a UK Business Ambassador, a member of the Trilateral Commission and a member of the GLF Global Leadership Foundation.

Dick is a past non executive director of Reuters and Thomson Reuters.

Dick is married with two daughters and five grandchildren. His interests include education, sailing, ballet and fine arts.

CHAPTER ELEVEN

THE QUEEN AT JAMESTOWN - 2007

"The Queen and the United States -
Celebrating the ideals that bind us together"

On November 15, 2006, Her Majesty Queen Elizabeth II used the occasion of her annual speech marking the opening session of Parliament to make the announcement that commemoration planners had been anticipating for several years: "The Duke of Edinburgh and I look forward to our state visit to the United States of America in May 2007 to celebrate the 400th anniversary of the Jamestown settlement."

With those thirty unadorned words uttered across the sea, planning for America's 400th Anniversary suddenly entered a dramatic new phase. The news of the British monarch's participation – punctuated with the poignant mention that it would be a reprise of her first state visit to the United States fifty years earlier for Jamestown's 350th anniversary commemoration – was flashed across the country, creating palpable excitement and electrifying preparations for anniversary-year observances. There now was no doubt that the Jamestown milestone would command international attention.

Britain's Queen Elizabeth and Prince Philip walk together through the Royal Gallery following her speech at the State opening of Parliament in the Palace of Westminster London, Wednesday Nov. 15 2006. AP Photo / Luke MacGregor

Queen Elizabeth II, Prince Philip, the Duke of Edinburgh, and Raymond Martinez, acting chief of protocol, walk down the red carpet at Richmond International airport Thursday May 3, 2007, in her first visit to the Virginia capital. AP Photo/Scott K. Brown

The Queen and Prince Philip are greeted at the front steps of Virginia's Executive Mansion by Governor Tim Kaine and First Lady Anne Holton.

On May 3, 2007, Queen Elizabeth II and Prince Philip flew directly from London to Richmond, and proceeded to the Executive Mansion for a brief reception hosted by Governor Kaine and First Lady Anne Holton and attended by five former Virginia governors and Senator John Warner.

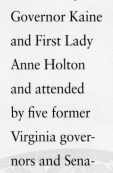

The crowd estimated at 20,000 gathered in and around the Capitol grounds to greet Her Majesty.

The royal couple then greeted members of the public during a stroll from the Mansion to the east lawn of Capitol Square, where she met the chiefs of the eight state-recognized Indian tribes and viewed a native American ceremonial dance. The Queen, Prince Phillip, and the Kaines then climbed the steps of the newly restored Virginia Capitol and waved to the assembled thousands from the south portico before entering the seat of government originally designed by Thomas Jefferson, the Commonwealth's second governor and, ironically, a foremost foe of monarchism. Entering the chamber of the House of Delegates, which traces its lineage to Jamestown's first representative assembly in 1619, the Queen received a rousing welcome and desk-thumping display of affection from Virginia's 21st-century lawmakers, who convened in a Special Joint Session for the occasion. She concluded her address by paying tribute to the special bond that unites Americans and Britons:

After Virginia's Native American tribal groups greeted Her Majesty and performed a ceremonial dance at the entrance to the Capitol, the Queen walks past Steve Adkins,

"This four hundredth anniversary marks a moment to recognise the deep friendship which exists between our two countries. Friendship is a complex concept. It means being able to debate openly, disagree on occasion, surmount both good times and bad, safe in the knowledge that the bonds that draw us together – of history, understanding,

Her Majesty, Governor Kaine, Prince Phillip and Judge Holton walk on the Capitol's portico to enter the Capitol flanked by members of Virginia Military Institute's Corps of Cadets (left) and Virginia Tech's Corps of Cadets (right).

Britain's Queen Elizabeth II, escorted by Governor Kaine, walks between rows of Virginia Indians at the Capitol on May 3, 2007 before making an address to the Virginia General Assembly in Richmond, the first stop of her six-day visit to the US. AP Photo/ Fiona Hanson

and warm regard – are far stronger than any temporary differences of opinion. The people of the United Kingdom have such a relationship with the people of this great nation. It is one of the most durable international collaborations anywhere in the world at any time in history, a friendship for which I certainly in my lifetime have had good cause to be thankful. That is a lasting legacy of Jamestown, that is something worth commemorating, and that is why I am pleased to be here today."

During her tour of the Capitol, Her Majesty visited with many distinguished guests, including famous civil rights activist Oliver W. Hill, Sr.

Her Majesty's speech in the House of Delegates Chamber

plauded by many local, national, and international officials

Richard Virgurra

Queen Elizabeth II waves as she and Prince Philip acknowledge the crowd during their carriage ride down Duke of Gloucester Street in Colonial Williamsburg, Va., Thursday evening, May 3, 2007. AP Photo/Adrin Snider, Pool

From Richmond, the royal entourage hastened to Duke of Gloucester Street in Colonial Williamsburg, where they traveled by horse-drawn carriage down the picturesque colonial avenue to the acclaim of thousands of cheering onlookers, and on to the nearby Williamsburg Inn, where the Queen and her retinue retired for the evening. The stately Inn had played host to Her Majesty fifty years earlier, and its most impressive suite, named in her honor, bore stunning photographs of the 32-year-old monarch that had so enthralled Virginians in 1957.

The next morning, Queen Elizabeth II and Prince Philip toured Jamestown Settlement and Historic Jamestowne, accompanied by Vice President and Mrs. Cheney, Governor Kaine, Justice O'Connor and other dignitaries.

Her Majesty, Queen Elizabeth II, began her tour of the re-created fort at JamestownSettlement on May 4, 2007, accompanied by (from left to right) Virginia Governor Timothy M. Kaine, Vice President Richard B. Cheney, and Jamestown-Yorktown Foundation Executive Director Philip G. Emerson.

While at the fort, remarks were given by Vice President Cheney, former Supreme Court Justice Sandra Day O'Connor, and Virginia State Senator Tommy Norment (shown), Chair of the Jamestown Coordination Committee. A brief program featuring historic tableaus was presented.

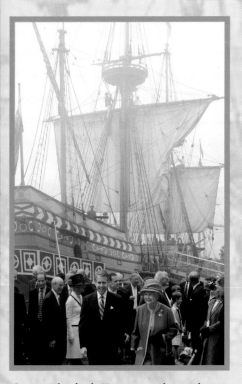

After viewing the ships, Queen Elizabeth and Prince Philip went their separate ways with the Prince lingering at the ships and then heading off with Joe Gutierrez, Curator of the Jamestown Yorktown Foundation, Mrs. Cheney and Virginia First Lady Anne Holton to visit other displays at the reconstructed fort.

Queen Elizabeth II is escorted past the "Susan Constant" ship by Philip Emerson, Executive Director of the Jamestown-Yorktown Foundation at Jamestown Settlement museum in Williamsburg, Va., Friday, May 4, 2007. The ship is a replica of one that brought America's first permanent colonists to Virginia in 1607.
AP Photo/Jim Young, Pool

Queen Elizabeth and Prince Phillip arrive on Jamestown Island and are greeted by officials from both
the National Park Service and the Association for the
Preservation for Virginia Antiquities who jointly man-
age the site. (APVA has since been renamed Preservation Virginia)

As the Queen's love for fresh flowers is widely known,
many smart young people brought flowers to the arrival
hoping they would catch the Queen's eye and she would
come over and speak – she often did.

Queen Elizabeth II listens to curator Beverly Straube as Vice President
Dick Cheney, left, looks on during a visit to the museum at Historic
Jamestowne, the site of Britain's first settlement in Virginia, Friday, May
4, 2007. AP Photo/Roger L. Wollenberg, pool

At the archeological site of the original Jamestown Fort, Historic
Jamestowne Chief Archeologist William Kelso talks to Her Majesty
Queen Elizabeth II about recent discoveries along with staff members from the APVA. The Queen later talked about how she and
others had unknowingly trod across the site of the original fort on
her visit in 1957.

In the background,
as the Queen chats
with fellow visi-
tors to the historic
site, Prince Philip,
accompanied by
Sandy Rives of
the National Park
Service, meets other
tourists.

Inside the Memorial Church on Jamestown Island, Her Majesty the Queen encourages Governor Timothy Kaine to try out the gift chair given to the people of the Commonwealth to commemorate her visit. The gift is hand crafted and dedicated to Bartholomew Gosnold, Captain of the God-speed. After leaving the historic church, National Park Service Representative and member of the federal Jamestown Commission Alexander Rives presents a gift to Her Majesty. Below, she is given a gift from the Jamestown Yorktown Foundation by its Chairman, State Senator Thomas Norment.

In the newly constructed state-of-the-art archeological lab, jointly run by Preservation Virginia and the National Park Service, Prince Philip gets a private tour of resources and research related to the discoveries made at the site of the original Jamestown Fort. The site was long thought lost - yet was discovered by archaeologist Bill Kelso in 1994. Mrs. Cheney, wife of Vice President Cheney and an accomplished historian in her own right, can be seen accompanying Prince Philip.

Inside the President's House at the College of William and Mary, the Queen is greeted by US Supreme Court Justice Anthony Kennedy and former Supreme Court Justice (and William and Mary Chancellor) Sandra Day O'Connor and President of the College Gene Nichol.

The Queen was made an honorary member of the Class of 2007 and was given the honor of having the Wren Bell ring in her honor - a tradition usually reserved for graduating seniors.

The Queen is introduced to the crowd from the piazza of the Wren Building - left to right Michael Powell, the Rector of the College, President Gene Nichol, Queen Elizabeth and Gov. Tim Kaine.

94

A reception followed at the Governor's Palace in Colonial Williamsburg, where federal and state commemoration leaders and other guests were formally presented to the Queen.

After exchanging toasts with the Governor at a tented luncheon beside the Governor's Palace gardens the Queen proceeded to the College of William and Mary, where she was made an honorary member of the Class of 2007 and rang the Wren Bell, an honor traditionally reserved for graduating seniors.

Before returning to London, the royal party made its way to Louisville for the Kentucky Derby and to Washington, D.C. for a state dinner hosted by President Bush and a wreath-laying at the new World War II memorial. A genuinely warm and often robust welcome, beamed nationally and internationally through wall-to-wall news coverage, greeted the British sovereign at every stop on her tour. In the wake of an American visit that some commentators speculated might be the last of her reign, Queen Elizabeth II left a deep reservoir of goodwill and affection, along with heightened awareness of Jamestown's importance as the place where America began four centuries ago.

In a tent erected for the occasion in the Garden of the restored Governor's Palace of Colonial Williamsburg, the Queen makes brief remarks at a garden luncheon attended by 300 people. This is the same site where, 50 years earlier, a reception was held for the Queen on her first visit to Jamestown. Seated at the head table are Virginia First Lady Anne Holton, Colonial Williamsburg President Colin Campbell, Virginia Governor Timothy Kaine, Williamsburg Mayor Jeanne Zeidler, Vice President Cheney, Former Justice Sandra Day O'Connor, Nancy Campbell, a member of the federal Jamestown Commission, and Mrs. Cheney. AP Photo/Steve Helber

KARENNE WOOD

Karenne Wood is an enrolled member of the Monacan Indian Nation. She directs the award-winning Virginia Indian Heritage Program at the Virginia Foundation for the Humanities and is a PhD candidate and Ford Fellow in anthropology at the University of Virginia, working to revitalize indigenous languages and cultural practices and to revise American Indian content in statewide educational resources. She has worked at the National Museum of the American Indian as a researcher.

Wood held a four-year gubernatorial appointment as Chair of the Virginia Council on Indians. She is the author of Markings on Earth, which won the North American Native Authors Award for Poetry in 2000, and she recently contributed a chapter on Southeastern Indians for National Geographic's reference book, Indian Nations of North America. In 2009 she spoke at a United Nations' Permanent Forum on Indigenous Issues event on "The Politics of Writing."

H. Edward Mann

THE FUTURE OF THE SPECIAL RELATIONSHIP

In 1946, Sir Winston Churchill spoke of a "special relationship" between the United States and Great Britain. This phrase has become something of a tradition, a part of the lexicon of British and American interactions. Though used frequently, it is like British common law – one would be hard-pressed to locate a precise definition. The "special relationship" has been used by many British and American policy makers as a point of justification and support for key policy decisions; and conversely, it has been used in deride policies and/or actions by politicians inconsistent with the "special relationship."

What then should we make of this term, and is it one that has relevance?

In 2011 U.S. President Barack Obama reiterated many of the same points that Churchill had made nearly 65 years earlier when the President addressed the British Parliament in the Great Hall at Westminster Hall in London. Speaking to the application of these guiding principles, the President quoted Sir Winston Churchill when he said, "the...Magna Carta, the Bill of Rights, Habeas Corpus, trial by jury, and English common law find their most famous expression in the American Declaration of Independence." The President reminded the world, once again, of the now centuries-long link between the United States and Great Britain and the shared commitment to democratic values and the ongoing efforts by both nations to serve as role models for similar, burgeoning efforts around the world.

Myriad instances in both American and British history belie both the intention and spirit of the democratic laws and principles which purport to undergird the governing systems of each nation. One need look no further than the institutions of slavery that were once prominent in both nations, to see that both have administered "democracy" inconsistently in the past.

Many of our respective leaders, indeed, founders of our respective democratic systems have behaved in ways that cause even our own citizens, let alone those of other nations, to search for consistency among the individual leaders and the ideas they espoused.

Bad manners are certainly have long been commonplace among the politicians and politics of the two nations. Keep in mind, the two nations have fought two wars AGAINST one another.

American politicians have, throughout our history, have spoken of monarchical government, generally, with contempt and have derisively referred to their political opponents or opposing parties as princely, or kingly or the like. And yet, Americans stood in line to catch a glimpse of Queen Elizabeth when she visited the United States in 2007. Tens of millions more, watched in rapt exhilaration when Prince William married Kate Middleton in 2011.

Kindness and gentility between or among our peoples have not served as the defining characteristic of the "special relationship." What then is it?

The most graphic manifestations of the British and American collaboration have been the military alliances formed between Great Britain and the U.S. over the past 100 years, leading to the current effort to fight global terrorism. As members of the Allied forces in World War I and World War II, the militaries of the two nations worked together to stop the rise of corrupt nationalism and fascism. Although US and British troops were not engaged in conflict together in the field, joint tactics, deployments and operations beginning with the Berlin Airlift in 1948-49 and continuing through the end of the Cold War in the 1980s were vital in curtailing the spread of communism.

New alliances, as embodied by joint task forces coordinated through NATO, give the US and UK, together with other democratic countries the capabilities needed to meet new threats -- threats like terrorism and piracy, cyber-attacks and the use of nuclear weapons by either rogue states, terrorist organizations or individual terrorists. Recent joint operations such as Iraqi Freedom, NATO support for Libyan rebels, and peacekeeping efforts with the United Nations, have thus far thwarted widespread anarchy and totalitarianism.

President Obama summarized the role of the two nations with a straightforward and powerful line:

"We are the nations most willing to stand up for the values of tolerance and self-determination"

In the 21st century, there is hope for expanded use of tactics beyond armed response and reflecting a shift towards 'soft power' rather than the hard power of military action. Yet the challenges that need to be addressed are sometimes extremely complicated and politically sensitive. As borders between countries become more porous, and with increasingly transient populations, a nations' security is only one reason for precise determination of the citizenship of specific individuals. Shared values now replace traditional ethnic and cultural ties. Yet with increasingly diverse religious, institutional and historic backgrounds, citizens in democratic countries become increasingly challenged to facilitate a common ground for political debate and dialogue. Both the UK and the United States have experienced the tragic consequences of citizens and/or illegal aliens who have not been inculcated to shared values and standards. The September 2001 attack on the US and the July 2005 bombings in London demonstrate that attacks being only instigated by clearly defined enemies from outside one's borders are a thing of the past. Therefore, nation-states need to do a better job of defining the terms of immigration – keeping doors open to those who seek a better life while impeding those who would seek to destroy their host.

When Churchill referred to the "special relationship" he did so in the following context: "Neither the sure prevention of war, nor the continuous rise of world organization will be gained without what I have called the fraternal association of the English-speaking peoples. This means a special relationship between the British Commonwealth and Empire and the United States." (Westminster College, Fulton, Missouri, in March 1946 - more commonly called the Iron Curtain speech.)

In other words, Churchill suggested solidarity exists among nations because of their shared democratic values and, further, that the preservation of democratic institutions in both nations, indeed, throughout other parts of the world as well, could not proceed by unilateral action alone, but would do so only to the extent that British and Americans were united and that mutually-beneficial efforts toward peace proceeded conjointly.

Two other threats to democracy include apathy and indifference and there is strong evidence of both in the United States and Great Britain. A New York Times headline from May 2011 reported that fewer than half of American eighth graders who took a recent National Assessment of Educational Progress knew the purpose of the Bill of Rights, and only one in 10 demonstrated acceptable knowledge of the checks and balances among the legislative, executive and judicial branches. At the same time, three-quarters of high school seniors were unable to demonstrate skills like identifying the effect of United States foreign policy on other nations or naming a power granted to Congress by the Constitution. In response, Sandra Day O'Connor, the former Justice of the U.S. Supreme Court, stated "we have a crisis on our hands when it comes to civics education. "We face difficult challenges at home and abroad," Justice O'Connor said in a statement. "Meanwhile, divisive rhetoric and a culture of sound bites threaten to drown out rational dialogue and debate. We cannot afford to continue to neglect the preparation of future generations for active and informed citizenship."

Yet the crisis is not only an American problem. The riots that started in London and raged across England in August of 2011 exposed an alienated disaffected youth culture that was bored and uncommitted to the values of its homeland. During an emergency debate in the House of Lords, The Archbishop of Canterbury Dr. Roland Williams said the riots represented "a breakdown of the sense of civic identity, shared identity, and shared responsibility".

"Over the last two decades, many would agree that our educational philosophy at every level has been more and more dominated by an instrumentalist model; less and less concerned with a building of virtue, character and citizenship," he said.

Establishing a democratic form of government is, itself, an arduous endeavor; and sustaining such a system is require eternal vigilance. Indeed, democracy does not survive on words alone. To endure, requires a commitment from every new and succeeding generation not only the underlying principles upon which the system was founded, but, as important, to maintaining and strengthening the system. At any given moment in time, democratic governance is a perishable item, the health of which is directly reflective of effort, or lack thereof, put into preserving it. If ignored, left unattended, it can grow stale and putrid with lack of attention; replaced all too easily by systems that are less demanding of the public's attention.

The need for civic education has been the concern of writers and political thinkers for thousands of years. Plato expanded upon the idea of a duty to our fellow citizens, expressed by the Latin word 'communitas' – commonly thought to mean merely a group of citizens in close proximity, sharing goals and aspirations. Yet Plato argued that in its fullest sense, communitas involves sacrifices and involvement on the part of an individual – and these sacrifices elevate the individual and enhance the well-being of the entire group. Democratic process - wherever it is utilized - is more than just a process. It is a symbol of a trust that citizens can work together to make a better world.

To maintain the process of democracy there needs to be a focus on exciting and innovative educational methodologies that promote the value of politics and the importance of civic engagement. Government works better when politics works better, and politics works better when citizens are informed and involved participants. Therefore, both the US and the UK need to encourage citizens to actively participate in the political process and government; evaluate and promote the best practices in civic education not only for students K-12 but for citizens of all ages.

Outreach to international audiences also need to be expanded. Over the past few years, the U.S. State Department and the British Foreign Ministry have encouraged governmental and non-governmental organizations to develop programs to facilitate citizen-to-citizen activism and dialogue in emerging democracies around the world. Supported by governmental agencies such as the National Endowment for Democracy and the British Westminster Foundation, many of these programs identify groups of international citizens to participate in workshops either in the U.S. or in their home country and consist of immersion programs that promote the core aspects of citizen engagement within democratic societies. The focus is on:

- Building civic participation skills and encourage public advocacy through peaceful and productive means;

- Identifying effective tools for and avenues of civic engagement;

- Promoting strategic and policy dialogue between government practitioners and marginalized populations;

- Establishing networking opportunities among democracy outreach programs

The challenges to preserve and foster democracy around the world are daunting – but there are new institutions tools and personalities to facilitate promote democratic institutions. Ironic perhaps to some, the renewed interest in the British monarchy, due in part to the Queens' Diamond Jubilee celebration, as well as the April 2011 marriage of the Prince William and Kate Middleton, create real opportunities to showcase democratic values around the world. Their charisma and youthful enthusiasm provide an opportunity for new personalities to inspire the next generation to rally around shared democratic beliefs as they take on the role as symbols of 1) the British royal family and 2) the continuity of Anglo American friendship and values. The fact is the reign of Queen Elizabeth II has served as a testament to the principles of democracy.

U.S. President George W. Bush, stated on May 14 2007 - the 400th anniversary of the settlement of Jamestown - "Today democratic institutions are taking root in places where liberty was not imaginable long ago. At the start of the 1980s, there were only 45 democracies on Earth. There are now more than 120 democracies, and more people live in freedom than ever before…. [O]ur shared respect for the rule of law and our deeply held belief in individual liberty … are more than just American values and British values, or Western values. They are universal values that come from a power greater than any man or any country. These values took root at Jamestown four centuries ago. They have flourished in our land, and one day they will flourish in every land."

Our "special relationship" hasn't always succeeded in leading us in the right or even the same direction. But, fundamentally, we are guided by a shared belief in self-governance, and dedication to the principals of freedom and opportunity for ALL people. It is in the optimism of people who look out at the horizon and believe that tomorrow can be an even better day not only for our own respective peoples, but for people around the world.

There could not have been a more sobering example of the fragility of societal institutions than the terrorist attacks that have ensued around the world over past decade. Such attacks force conscientious people to realize just how much about society and the nation is taken for granted – that things once regarded as solid, permanent, and unwavering are in fact only as strong as the effort we put into building and protecting them. The same may be said of democracy.

The Arab Spring suggests ample evidence that despite it shortcomings and imperfections, democracy is preferred over other forms of government that limit personal freedoms and curtail individual opportunity.

As America begins a new century, every citizen committed to strengthening democratic principles must renew his or her pledge to responsible civic education – fostering a nationwide commitment to ensuring that Americans are taught and encouraged to become actively engaged in civic life. To do anything less jeopardizes the foundations of a free and self-governing society.

If democracy and the process of self-government are to endure and thrive, particularly among nations that are clamoring for change, democratic governments must stress the value and importance of civic engagement.

"The future is, as ever, obscure. The only certainty is that it will present the world with new and daunting problems, but if we continue to stick to our fundamental ideals, I have every confidence that we can resolve them. All our history in this and earlier centuries underlines the basic point that the best progress is made when Europeans and Americans act in concert. We must not allow ourselves to be enticed into a form of continental insularity. I believe this is particularly important now, at a time of major social, environmental, and economic changes in your continent, and in Asia and Africa. We must make sure that those changes do not become convulsions."

Her Majesty Queen Elizabeth II

A Special Celebration for a Special Relationship

And a Hopeful Future

2012 is the year in which the world celebrates the sixty years Her Majesty Queen Elizabeth II has been on the throne of Great Britain. Of British monarchs, only Queen Victoria ruled longer. On the global stage, only two other rulers - Emperor Hirohito of Japan (who ruled from 1923 -1986) and King Bhumibol Adulyadej of Thailand (1946 -) have reached this level of longevity.

The affection and friendship which Her Majesty has for the United States is evinced by her many trips over the years "across the pond" whether on affairs of state, or on those occasions when she sought to gain insights related to horse racing, her favorite personal passion. Americans enthusiastically return this admiration, demonstrated by the parades and throngs of well-wishers that greet her, by the high degree of respect given her as Queen, and by the sense of appreciation for her celebration of the shared values – democracy, rule of law, free enterprise, diversity, language and culture - that the two countries hold dear.

Looking to the future, Her Majesty no doubt takes great pleasure in knowing that the 'special relationship' she has so carefully stewarded is founded on important values that continue to spread across the globe. During 1976, on her visit to the United States to celebrate the bicentennial of American Independence, there were only 45 democracies on earth. In 2012, there are over 120 - and more people live in freedom than ever before. One day her responsibilities will be entrusted to a younger generation, yet she can rest assured that she has strengthened the unique heritage that forever link Great Britain and the United States of America.

Prince William, Duke of Cambridge and Catherine, Duchess of Cambridge, formerly known as Kate Middleton, arrive to the 'BAFTA Brits to Watch' gala in Los Angeles, California. Photo Credit: Krista Kennell/Sipa via AP Images

ACKNOWLEDGEMENTS

Many individuals offered advice and made suggestions for the betterment of this volume. The publisher and co-editors wish to thank them, the authors who contributed essays, as well as the following individuals and groups for providing photographs and additional assistance.

Editorial assistance

National Park Service, US Department of Interior; United States Supreme Court (Linda Neary); The University of Virginia Center for Politics, (Larry J. Sabato, Director, and Ken Stroupe, Chief of Staff); Frank Atkinson, Chair of the Jamestown 400th Commemoration Commission; Mark Womble at BAE Systems; Phil Emerson and Debbie Padgett at the Jamestown Yorktown Foundation; the College of William and Mary; The Library of Virginia (Papers of Governor Mills E. Godwin); The Jefferson Library at Monticello; Preservation Virginia, The Colonial Williamsburg Foundation, The British Jamestown Committee (Lord Alan Watson and Sir Robert Worcester, Co-chairs) and all members of The Jamestown 400th Commemoration Commission, including Commissioner Michael Gleason for use of a portion of an essay from the December 19th 2006 Commemorative Program; and Horace Williams Mann for his research efforts – primarily identifying sources for photos - and his good humor.

Photos

Unless captioned near the respective illustration, photos came from a myriad of archive resources, including:

The Library of Virginia; The British Library; The British Museum; The Ashmolean Museum of Art and Archeology at Oxford University; The Smithsonian Institution; Dementi Family Archives, The British Jamestown Committee and the Jamestown 400th Commemoration Commission (Photos taken in England by Nicolas Bell); The National Portrait Gallery (London); The College of William and Mary (Amy Schindler, University Archivist, Special Collections, Earl Gregg Swem Library); Jamestown Yorktown Foundation; Library of Virginia, Virginia Chamber of Commerce Collection; Lewis Malon and Catherine Dean at Preservation Virginia, The Library of the University of Virginia.

Specific acknowledgements to those intrepid photographers who contributed to the chapter on the Queen's Visit in 2007:

Her Majesty addressing the General Assembly, Her Majesty entering the Capitol, Her Majesty with
   Oliver Hill, Sr., - Bob Brown, Richmond Times-Dispatch;
Her Majesty sitting in the Old House Chamber - M. T. Cavanaugh, European Press Association;
Royal Party at the Governor's Mansion - Michaele White, Photographer for the Governor of Virginia;
Her Majesty on walkabout - Joe Mahoney, Richmond Times-Dispatch;
General Assembly applauding Her Majesty - Steve Helber, Associated Press ;
The National Park Service, (multiple photographers coordinated through Public Affairs Manager Mike Litterest
   and Superintendent Dan Smith at Colonial Historical National Park);
The College of William and Mary – Office of Strategic Initiatives - Creative Services (Tina Coleman)